EDITED BY MARCUS HARRISON GREEN

Emerald Reflections: A South Seattle Emerald _Anthology_

FLY TO THE ASSEMBLIES!

Seattle and the Rise of the Resistance

edited by

Marcus Harrison Green

Afterword by

Mark Baumgarten

3

Edited by Marcus Harrison Green

Cover art: © Vladimir Verano

Book and cover design: Vladimir Verano, Third Place Press

978-1-60944-116-6

Published in the United States by
Third Place Press
17171 Bothell Way NE
Lake Forest Park, WA 98155

press@thirdplacebooks.com

Please contact the publisher for Library of Congress Catalog Data

This anthology was created in partnership with

Table of Contents

Foreword

That perilous times plague us was a fact underscored for many with the outcome of the 2016 presidential election.

For some, it forever shattered the faith they placed in this country and its institutions. For others, it simply reinforced the skepticism ever-present in their hearts about this American experiment.

The ensuing time brought a range of mourning, navel gazing, myth busting, blame assignment, and most profoundly valorous actions of those unwilling to acquiesce to the circumstance their country now faces.

In that vein, this collection of essays is not about the dreariness of what was, but the splendor of what can be in America.

These essays attempt to locate that future, and along the way help readers discover resolve, resilience, and most of all an illuminating hope. It is my wish that the words in this book have the enduring effect historian Howard Zinn's had on this writer the morning of November 9th, 2016, after something I believed was impossible had transpired:

> "TO BE HOPEFUL in bad times is not just foolishly romantic. It is based on the fact that human history is a history not only of cruelty, but also of compassion, sacrifice, courage, kindness.
>
> What we choose to emphasize in this complex history will determine our lives. If we see only the worst, it destroys our capacity to do something. If we remember those times and places—and there are so many—where people have behaved magnificently, this

gives us the energy to act, and at least the possibility of sending this spinning top of a world in a different direction.

And if we do act, in however small a way, we don't have to wait for some grand utopian future. The future is an infinite succession of presents, and to live now as we think human beings should live, in defiance of all that is bad around us, is itself a marvelous victory."

Choose hope, always.

Marcus Harrison Green

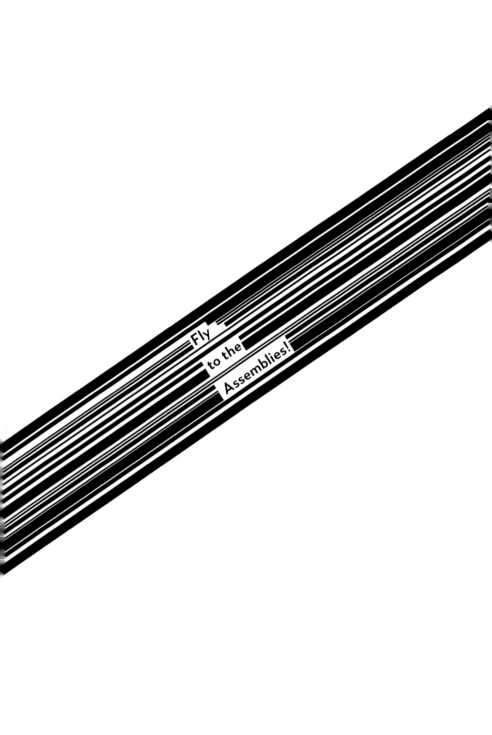
Fly to the Assemblies!

A Day Not Far

by Marcus Harrison Green

Since November, time has passed at the pace of erosion for the punch-drunk many. Days that have long arrived weighted down by decades of civic impoverishment now begin with additional fatigue brought on by the mental toll of our new political reality.

Months after the election, I still encounter my fellow distressed Americans, seemingly shipwrecked after experiencing the unfathomable. All have some variation of the same stream of questions: How do we mount a resistance to the evil around us? How do we find hope? How do we save this country?

But for me . . . for me, there's another question that assaults my brain at daybreak every morning, on that is no less agile in its evasion of easy answers: Is this country worth saving?

Daily, I see citizens that share my dark complexion killed on video under questionable circumstances, falling at the hands of those authorized to serve and protect. Fear follows, for my own life and those of my young nephews should they be stopped by law enforcement.

Weekly, I will see a report of some crazed gunman who has senselessly abandoned any attachment to humanity, ripping people from their lives in a mass execution.

Monthly, I witness more of our citizen's plummet into poverty, falling into destitution, spiraling into a bottomless pit of despair.

Yearly, I view the crisis to our climate go unaddressed.

Of course, our perilous times have not been without their cracks of daylight.

Philosopher Jean-Jacques Rousseau believed that in a genuine democracy, each citizen would be so consumed with the state of their republic that they would "fly to the assemblies," correcting any wrong foisted on the collective good. In the early months of the new administration, our republic saw people fly to the airports, fly to marches, and fly to the streets to defend their fellow citizens.

While those inspiring spurts have been welcome, most days since early November find me waiting for hope to prevail inside. Our present has put a lie to tales of hopes eternal springing.

I continue waiting for our current reality to cease the constant leeching of optimism from my spirit while I cling to every last drop for dear life.

I keep anticipating a restoration of a sane country, a sharp shift away from the absurd.

I fight the urge to throw dirt on the coffin of my belief in this society.

I try to deny that the love my fellow citizens have for this country could be overwhelmed by hatred of the other, and the unbridle interests of the self.

But all that I thought solid has melted into air, all that I thought holy is profaned.

And I know it is readily force fed to us over and over that there were valid reasons to endorse the presidency and platform of the person who now occupies the White House—but I'm rather tempted to say that doing the wrong thing for the right reasons still amounts to the wrong thing, and exempts no one from its consequences.

I try to resuscitate my sense of hope by remembering the spirit of those who came before me, the DNA coursing through my veins belonging to former slaves and natives who survived the inhumane horrors of a savage institution, and a merciless genocide committed in the name of a righteous destiny.

Yet even today I see the horrific ramifications from both American atrocities still lingering for a people who, yes, survive, but still find trouble fully *living* in our society.

Fully living in our society, free from oppression, free from persecution . . . free from fear.

It never dawned on me before that many of us were taking those entitled freedoms for granted, thinking them ours by default. But now we question the fragility of those freedoms for ourselves—facing an imminent danger of their disintegration.

In those first days of the administration I saw images of young men and women—legal residents of this country—being handcuffed at airports, their social media being reviewed by law enforcement who then interrogate them on their views of President Trump.

Americans, descended from Iran, Iraq and Somalia cried: *Not here! Not here! Never did I ever believe this could happen in this country!*

And yes, I know even today the resistance grows against these grave injustices. But even now that opposition is met by the persistence of those who believe their actions just and those who support them.

As Kellyanne Conway, Counselor to the president, said in those early days of the presidency: *Things are just getting started.*

I am reminded of a conversation I had with two young children—a young girl and young boy—who are tutored be me and my mother every week.

Both are American, but also Muslim, and of Somali descent.

Months ago they asked us, "Why, why does the new president hate us. We're scared of what will happen to our family."

I kept thinking, *God, even here, even now. . . . This moment will not allow the children their innocence.*

Our instinct was to wrap them up in our arms and flee, and as we fled, gathering up my LGBTQ+ brothers and sisters, sweeping up my cousins belonging to communities of color, and evacuating this country never to return.

I didn't want them to endure what I almost am certain they will. Treatment as abnormal citizens, hated for simply existing, the targets of a channeled, misplaced rage of those fearful of an evolving world.

I was tempted to say, "The hell with it," to look at the marches taking place in America's liberal strongholds, and shout, "Unless we have the same numbers in Alabama, Mississippi, Missouri, and Kansas"— which we didn't even during the unsuccessful protests of the Iraq war— "what good will it truly do?"

It was interesting then that I found resolve to press forward in the unlikeliest place: from a person who saw greatness where I saw horror, in a vision of a future containing echoes of primitive times.

I interviewed this man who identified as a patriot and fervent supporter of Donald Trump; who was able to perform enough moral contortions to see divine intervention in a man deemed a serial liar, narcissist, and sexual predator.

"Any person can be used as a vessel for good," he told me. "It can come from the most unlikeliest of people. America will be pro-life. I don't have to fear my guns being taken away, they'll be God in the schools, and terrorists won't attack us anymore."

He added: "Do you really think all of this is due to one man . . . happening because of one man? *No . . . and that's your problem, today was borne out of many todays of the past, out of a ceaseless commitment.*

"This is happening because of a commitment to an idea of who we are, the same **who we are** *is what we believe this country should be. And we've believed that through countless defeats, myriad ridicule, and a world we thought had turned against us."*

"Even now," he said, "even now, you rush to march; you resort to demanding anyone but Trump instead of someone forged from your unyielding beliefs, values and principles. How fragile those things become when you return to power.

"Your problem is you don't know who you are. Once you get power, then what? What is this world you truly want? Where is the affirmation of that world you seek? Hope and Change is one thing," he said. "That's easy

to convey but often fleeting. Precision and execution is quite another, harder, but ultimately more durable.

"Our day has arrived," he said, *"and we do not intend to relinquish it.*

"Spit on us, curse us, call us what you will, we're not afraid to be who are and do what we feel is right for this world. Our time is now. I never doubted this day would come."

While there was much he vomited forth that I found repugnant, some of his words echoed truth.

Because it is true that our current president is just a man and this is just one moment in our epoch. And all men and all moments, no matter how gruesome, come to their end. That isn't to trivialize what is anticipated to be a difficult time for many, induced by this presidency.

But it steers me clearly towards our future, asking just *who* is it that will emerge once this time is over—because all those forces that seemingly culminated in the rise of this president have been alive and well before him, and will be alive and well long after.

And as much as we want to avert our eyes to the wrecking ball currently ravaging our society, this moment is the most important of our lives, because it is the one we know we have. It is the one that has finally awakened so many from an apathetic slumber.

This is a moment to be seized, a time for collective reflection on *who* we've been as country and a society, to finally ask *who* we are now, and *who* exactly it is we wish to be.

This moment is one in which we can finally examine the truth, closely inspect our stated desire to remain aware of the persecution of all of America's kin. Now is the time to ask if our admonishments of equity for all, and radical love towards all will stand even after this oppressive Executive Branch falls.

People say now is the time to find hope, to find vision, and to establish a new doctrine for American society. I don't doubt that it is just that, but I know those things will never properly materialize without us first finding our collective character.

Because, to paraphrase Heraclitus, it is character that is our destiny. It is character that leads to truth. It is truth that serves as fuel for the flame that burns brighter than any evil, no matter its unique brand of wickedness.

And we must trumpet a character that blares so loudly it leaves no residuals from a past marked by slavery, genocide, anti-Semitism, and homophobia.

Who we are can be a country that embarks on an economic system that will never allow eight men to control more wealth than half the world's population.

Who we are can be a society that exempts no one from the glow of America's kindness, lavishing its civility on all of its citizenry; one where every unearned privilege subordinates itself to servicing the marginalized amongst us.

It is this *who we are* as a society that can demolish our current social architecture that was erected so long ago, the same one that holds in place floors of some and ceilings for others. We can replace it with an egalitarian social construction that leaves no one outside.

Who we are can be a people who call wrong for wrong no matter if it is conducted by a Democratic president overseeing drone strikes that kill innocent brown children, or a Republican president who seems the embodiment of incompetence run amok.

Who we are can be people who realize that there is no darkness so massive that itcannot be thwarted even by slivers of light—because love, though it may lose battles, will win wars.

Who we are can be people who, now awake, must be vigilant against slumber; an engaged, informed, skeptical citizenry ultimately impervious to lies and the liars who weaponize false claims, and alternative facts.

Who we are is so much more than one moment on one night during one early November.

Knowing who we are, we can write our future's history right now, today, this moment, this hour, this second, exchanging the status quo for what can be a future bereft of a past we were too scared to walk away from.

That conception of *who we are* is what persuaded me to stop taking imaginary flight with the children I tutor. It made me put them down, and clasp their hands as we walked together to face a future, armed with something greater than hope.

No, I found something much better than that passive emotion.

I found determination in my Muslim brother and sisters who continue to prove that unapologetically existing at this point in our nation's history is itself a fierce rebellion.

I found love, in communities of people who sacrifice their wages and their time and their stations in life to open their doors and hearts to people they would not have spoken two syllables to only months ago.

I found courage, in a past of marginalized and oppressed men, women, and gender non-conforming people who fought, bled, and died for imagining what we could be, even with no clear cut evidence at the that time things could be transformed—so that that we too can now imagine what we can be.

Because this is your country, this is my country, let that fact never be forgotten, never be taken for granted again, never be surrendered to those unwilling to acknowledge our ever-widening reservoir of justice.

There is no need to wait for a congress, a president, a messiah, nor an army because *who we are* is a choice we have the agency to make every single day we live.

And the day is coming when we will be *who we will be, who we can be, who we must become.* And on that day *who we are* will speak so loudly, will rumble so deeply inside the core of every citizen of this country, and beyond this country.

Rumble so deeply that our ethics, our compassion, our conscience won't require words for expression.

Our character will roar loudly enough.

That day will come, that day will reign. That day will triumph.

Let us make it so. . . . Let *us* make it so.

Make America Again

by *Ben Hunter*

My work revolves around looking to the past. Preparing for something like this brings me back to those that have spoken on this issue before me; in another place or another period of time. The philosophies from every elder before us whose watched and witnessed the ebb and flow of a nation created. The smell of the air, the sound of the wind, even the taste of things enhance or fade with the evolutions and devolutions of a growing society. I think of them and say thank you.

This country itself was founded at the dawn of a new period. The Age of Reason it was called. The Enlightenment, placing reason as the prime motivator for action, helping determine our current society through ideals of life, liberty, and the pursuit of happiness. Helping determine our country as a place for tolerance, equality, freedom. Fundamentally, that we are all treated as rational beings. That we all have the ability to self-determine, to have an identity, and allow that to shape our lives with the mold that fancies our passions and talents. To be an individual, to think for ourselves, work for ourselves, live for ourselves.

But right out of the gate, Americans engaged in the same type of social behavior from whence they came. Slavery and indentured servitude built this nation into the prosperous country that it is. This is fundamental when exploring the psyche of American politics and society. Because it identifies, at the root, the hypocrisy upon which this country has been founded. While racism is a towering problem in this country—and around the world—racism is implicitly folded into a larger discussion of class. This is what Dr. King spoke of. Because we aren't just fighting a war on racism, we are fighting for justice in all forms of oppression.

Since the formation of this country, it wasn't just Blacks and Native Americans getting trampled on, but anyone who wasn't a rich, white, male; a perspective that has written the entire narrative of this nation ever since. Alongside that narrative is this position of power, of privilege. So much so that it disallows, even now in 2017, the *idea* of putting anything other than white and male within the envelope of power. So that when we elect a Black president, we can shout out to the world how evolved we are, how progressive we are, the example that should be followed from the land of the free. Yet we can still lock up people of color at rates far higher than whites. We close down schools in low-income neighborhoods. We chalk up the price of good, healthy food, and allow the poor to feast on McDonalds and Pepsi.

Our establishment has never wanted to accept any other group as *powerful* for fear that it would defy the supposed truth that has been portrayed for hundreds of years. And as the decades go by, subtle and not so subtle tricks and tactics develop to curtail, disrupt, denigrate, and dismantle any movement that looks to empower themselves. Because sharing power is not the American way.

So when you tell people that they have self-determination, that they have an identity, that they can think and work and live for themselves, except when they're Black, or a woman, or gay, or poor, you insert into that person, or those persons the same kind of psychological disregard for each other. You instill inside them that same insidiousness, that same apathy, that same disregard for each other. That power can't be shared, but I can still exist as an individual.

This is what I see as our biggest folly. This is what I regard as our primary concern. Because it's more than race, or gender, or even class. It comes down to a position that has been curated by 500 years of false advertising. That individuality will give us life, liberty, and happiness.

That capitalist, self-determination will somehow produce a tolerant, and united society.

We built this nation only considering a small portion of the people that were a part of it. And now we are still grappling with that fundamental flaw, so much so that we don't know *how* to acknowledge others. And that the mechanism for bringing us together has pulled us apart. All of this technology has pulled us so far apart, that we now find more solace in talking to Siri than to a real person. We'd rather hear stories from our friends on Facebook and through Twitter than through conversation.

We can't acknowledge people if we don't know how to talk to them. We can't empathize with people if we only rely on emoticons.

Our senses are the only thing we have to guide us through this world. Instead, we've traded them in for an algorithm. We've put our trust in a robot of whose purpose is to give us what we want, so that all we know is getting what we want. We play video games that immerse us in war, so that we no longer have the perspective of a civilian. Our relationships are through a virtual reality that feeds our selfishness over our selflessness. It draws on our need to consume unnecessary products and things, over soulful and enlightening conversation. This emphasis on consumption affects the most vulnerable of minds, the most absorbent of minds, the most malleable of minds: those of our children.

We are what we see, and if this is what we feed our children than what else can we possibly expect out of them?! Are they not our future? Are they not our hopes and dreams? Are they not our legacy? What is the legacy of our children? What is the legacy of the United States?

I bring up acknowledgement because we don't know how to talk to each other anymore. We don't know how to have differing opinions without callousness. We don't know how to engage in debate without our teeth exposed. We're out for blood, yet we're supposed to collectively be striving for a better America for *everyone.*

Dr. King understood this on a profound level. He was a fierce opponent of the Vietnam war for not just what it did to our veterans, but for that false advertising. Promoting freedom by having people who are not free in America kill others that are not free elsewhere.

He said:

"And as I ponder the madness of Vietnam and search within myself for ways to understand and respond in compassion, my mind goes constantly to the people of that peninsula. I speak now not of the soldiers of each side, not of the ideologies of the Liberation Front, not of the junta in Saigon, but simply of the people who have been living under the curse of war for almost three continuous decades now. I think of them, too, because it is clear to me that there will be no meaningful solution there until some attempt is made to know them and hear their broken cries."

And are we still not caught up in that same war today in the middle-east? In parts of Africa. At home in North Dakota. Or Baltimore.

And so to *acknowledge*, means that we must alter our system of values.

Our current values are money and power. Our wars are based on money and power. Everything our government does has a bottom line, and it is what our social policy is based on, environmental policy is based on, education policy is based on. And if our policies are for the benefit of our country, through whom power is defined as rich, white, and male, how do we expect to create policy that is equitable and fair?

The first step of our mighty revolution must start with a redefinition of the values of our American and Global polity. We must draw lines in the sand, and say you can not and will not cross these lines. To cross these lines goes against our collective humanity. To cross these lines goes against the sanctity of our creed as Americans.

To do this isn't easy. To do this is to go against a machine that was built and has been recalibrated over and over to combat our collectivism, to combat our empathy and connection and reliance and trust in one another. To do this we must challenge the system with which we live, but we must challenge it going back to our founding. The building blocks that our founding fathers were determined to construct this country with were fundamentally sound. Life, liberty, and the pursuit of happiness. Built on Reason. It wasn't that our individuality was better than our collective, but that our collective was made stronger through our distinctness and our uniqueness. And that our love for each other would fortify that individuality.

We have come to the precipice that is our now. We have come to that moment where another period must start and we must recalibrate. The fierce urgency of now is upon us, and it requires the only type of force that can withstand the mechanisms of division. That force must be love. But don't get me twisted, because this love isn't unicorns and pink roses. It's not just holding hands, or singing songs. This love is backbone. This love is a fire down below. This love is a juggernaut. This love is a steel chain linking our histories, our cultures, our colors, our futures.

Dr. King said:

> "When I speak of love I am not speaking of some sentimental and weak response. I am not speaking of that force which is just emotional bosh. I am speaking of that force which all of the great religions have seen as the supreme unifying principle of life."

I read this over and over, because something about that seemed so right and true, but also unsettling. The *supreme unifying principle of life. All the great religions.*

I met up with a friend who talked to me about growing up Muslim. He said, "there are 1.5 billion Muslims, some brown, some black, men, women, and none of them get along. If we could all just decide to join hands we could do anything".

Why is it so hard for us to harness this love, this supreme unifying principle of life?

I went to South Dakota in September with my sweetheart to bring food and supplies and stand in solidarity with Standing Rock—more than 200 sovereign nations coming together to support each other, to protect each other, to protect the water. We spent the days working, organizing donations and lending a hand where were needed, and spent the night around a great fire listening to stories and songs, watching dances, and being part of this unifying principle, this unwavering force of Love. A love that worked together and stood side-by-side to protect what's sacred. A love that laughed, sang, and danced together to feed what's sacred. A love that welcomed anybody that believed in the values of that Love.

When we say we need to change our values, we are engaging in a commitment to establish better relationships—a relationship with ourselves, our neighbors, our earth, and our sky. Our love must be a relationship. A relationship fortified by our senses.

To see the valleys and the mountains. To look in each other's eyes.

To taste the spices and flavors that make up our vast collection of cultures from the diverse regions around the world.

To listen to the wind and the thunder. To hear our voices and rhythms and music.

To feel the warmth of the sun or the soft morning rain. To feel the touch of a loved one.

To smell the flowers, the food, or a person's scent.

Our love must be rooted in our senses, because that is how we acknowledge each other, and that is how we acknowledge this earth.

Our country must be founded on the idea that we all count. At the moment only a few count. But it's not because we don't have the capacity to love, but that we've been groomed not to. We must Make America Again, in the way that it was meant to be.

The how is the tough part. The how can be done in many ways, within our current system, and outside of it.

Already there are people and groups developing new ways to co-exist, instead of the rising cost of isolation in many apartment complexes. Novel ways to run a business so that more people have ownership of their work. Creative alternatives to teach and learn so that children don't fall through the cracks of school systems that don't meet their needs. Revisiting traditional farming techniques that yield organic, healthy food that take care of our land, and re-instill pride and respect to our farmers. These things are all being done outside of our government. These things are being done by grassroots efforts, by small communities thinking of new ideas to tackle these systems of oppression.

At the same time there are more women and people of color in state and national office than ever before, allowing more voices and representation in our government. Because we need black and brown brothers and sisters in office. We need LGBTQ people in office. We need people in office that represent our constituency, or else that power remains, rich, male, and white.

It's important that we marry both of these strategies. It's important that we organize, and rally beside each other. It's important that we express ourselves and be heard, that we engage in activities and hobbies that pique our interests, our passions, while also advancing our independent and collective culture. And it's okay to be angry; rather, it's important to be angry to remind us that we have souls, and minds, and hearts, and self-determination.

Dr. King said,

"These are the times for real choices and not false ones. We are at the moment when our lives must be placed on the line if our nation is to survive its own folly. Every man of humane convictions must decide on the protest that best suits his convictions, but we must all protest."

We need to stop looking down, or looking at screens, or allowing our headphones to deafen us to the sounds around us. We must be aware to be alive. And we must acknowledge to be acknowledged.

The Rural America That is Part of Me

by Irene DeMaris

I moved to Seattle in 2008 and it rocked my world. To understand why, I need to share a little about my life before the Emerald City.

I grew up in a small town, and then matriculated to college in another small town, thinking I'd end up in a smaller big town (Portland). Diversity was the one African-American, and Latino family in my school.

My own family was a mix of farmers, blue collar workers, and my college educated parents. My family landed in this town because my mother grew up in rural America, and even though my dad was a Seattleite, he had worked summers on the family farm in rural America and loved living off the land. My grandparents' parents were all farmers; thinking of them gave me a constant dose of humility.

Garfield, Washington was where my mom grew up. She graduated with less than twenty people in this town surrounded by the rolling fields of the Palouse. Tradition in Garfield was to graduate and then go to college. In fact, those with farming backgrounds went to learn business so they could better run their farms as many were expected to return home to continue the family businesses.

Those who did return, mainly the men, came home married with college educated women. My mom's returning classmates worked hard. She even spoke to me about one farming family who went to Washington, D.C. to represent the community, lobbying for farm subsidies when prices for lentils, wheat, and barley plummeted. My mom's peers were—and are—smart and savvy, but the plant closed & so did the grocery store. This preceded quite a few restaurants trying to open but quickly shutting their doors again.

Now no one really goes back to Garfield these days and I remember witnessing its decline throughout my childhood. The Garfield School District that my grandfather was the proud superintendent of is now defunct, merging with districts of smaller towns.

A way of life has ended; abundance has been replaced by scarcity because there are no more jobs. Yet, as my mom was quick to remind me, the stereotype of uneducated Americans in rural areas is false because throughout the 60s, 70s, and 80s college was affordable for all; "politically savvy adults populate these declining communities".

I grew up split between Brush Prairie and Ridgefield, Washington located in Clark County—home of Vancouver. Although it's in close proximity to Portland, it was an overwhelmingly red county. When we speak of the people in America who voted for Trump, I know them. They are the faces I keep seeing, especially the 53 percent of white women, unlike me, who voted for Trump.

Back to small town girl moves to the big city. When I moved to Seattle after years of pushing back against Republicans in my classes, it was refreshing. For the first time in my life, I felt I could voice my political views without being personally attacked. I moved to the North End of Seattle and remained there until moving to Hillman City, in South Seattle, in 2014. As my mom recently reminded me, I was with like-minded progressive individuals. I forgot my roots.

My life changed when I moved to South Seattle. In theory I was a very progressive person, yet, I had been so isolated for most of my life it took time to really sit with the fact that I had and have more privilege than I can understand. It took me leaving my small town and venturing from the comfort of North Seattle. Many people never leave rural America or frequent places where their skin complexion is scarce.

Ignorance is bliss and I find it hard to say that people in rural America do not know what is going on, yet, I cannot squarely put the blame on rural America for what has happened in our country. Time and time again, our patriarchal systems have siloed America into different groups. Historically this has proven true, time and time again.

I believe that the Republican base has played into the fears of rural America, keeping them in an unjust system while feeding them lies. As the urban and other areas of America embraced the intersectionality of life, that we are all connected, rural America is disconnected and forgotten.

Growing up, my mom says life was very insular. Though she was aware of current events, many of them outside of her town could have been taking place in another country. The disconnect felt by so many is real and more tangible to the rest of us now.

My ties to rural America are part of my DNA and I had forgotten. I had pushed back the memories of growing up in a red county, and unfortunately I remembered too late. I am far from enlightened, but this election has brought me to my knees and humbled me.

It's not okay. I am safe thanks to my unearned white privilege, but countless others are not. I worry for my friends who aren't white, middle class, straight, Christians because the next phase of America isn't about hope or being stronger together, it's based in the fear of a scarcity that does not exist.

Our patriarchy systems must be dismantled, yet I find myself drawn to a rural America that is also trapped in the myth of scarcity, pain, and has been economically bludgeoned. How do we show compassion when something truly terrible has happened? That's when it is time for people to do what we say when we claim the title ally.

It's okay to be angry; it's okay to mourn a bit longer. However, it's not okay for allies to expect the groups we claim alignment with to be the ones to reach out and be compassionate to rural America. It's people who look like me and have the same unearned privileges to do so. I can choose compassion because it's safe for me to do so. Hearts and minds need to be changed in rural America and that's going to take time.

We cannot make America great without all of America. It's going to take all hands on deck, and even more so, it's going to take rural America waking up.

Entering the holiday season, as hard as it can be to swallow, maybe those of us coming home to rural America need to take the time to listen and find the deeper issue, and find compassion—if not Thanksgiving, then maybe Christmas, or even Easter.

Build up your relationships with rural America and show them the beauty that is possible in America. Change hearts and open minds. That's how we change the system, we must all be connected.

We Must Aim Higher

by Dustin Washington

I know many are hurt and scared right now but this election clarifies where we are as a country. I appreciate the honesty of this election. Honesty is a gift. Honesty destroys all illusions.

Honesty calls us to step into our individual and collective power. *If* you are awake, you will receive the deeper message of this moment in time. We always seek someone else to blame, but if you could see deep enough, you would see that this is a reflection on *all* of us. A reflection of us being out of our power and not having vision.

If you didn't know how deep racism is in this country, now you do. If you didn't know how dark the shadow of America was and is, now you do. Us being able to see the shadow and the Racism of this country is a gift.

The truth is Trump built a movement. A sick, racist and hateful movement, but it was a movement. A movement always wins. It's Time *we* build *our* movement. Hillary may have been a "better choice" than Trump but she wasn't the choice we truly needed.

She would have continued the same basic neo-liberal, globalist, violent and racist status quo agenda. We must set our sights higher, much higher than *not* electing a Trump or electing a Clinton, to hell with that.

This is an opportunity for us to step out of the box, out of the matrix of what we believe is possible and begin to not only imagine the world we really want but to embark on the journey to build that world. Another world *is* possible. Do you believe?

Having a Bull Connor type figure (aka Trump) could be a galvanizing force for a People's movement. If we step into our Power and stop with the bullshit. This is a call from the Creator for us to step into our Power.

The Universe reflected back to us what we most need in this moment in history. None of us can see the future but we can shape the future. The question is will we/you seize this moment?

Will you just moan and complain or will you be a part of building the real New World Order, the Order of Justice and Love.

I know I will.

I Have No Grace Today

by Kristin Leong

> *"To all of the little girls who are watching this, never doubt that you are valuable and powerful and deserving of every chance and opportunity in the world to pursue and achieve your own dreams."*
>
> ~Hillary Clinton, the most qualified person ever to run for president of the United States of America, who also happens to be a woman who lost the election (but not the popular vote).

Tell little girls whatever you want about their worth and potential, but this country just showed them who's boss. And it's not them. And it's not any one spray-tanned megalomaniac either. It's fear and hate.

Donald Trump doesn't scare me. He's all fluffy hair and gold toilets and mail-order steaks. Whatever.

It's the people who scare me. The ones in red hats but also the ones who didn't vote. The ones who threw away their vote in protest. All those white women who considered their options and decided, yes, I will vote for a man who defended himself against a flood of sexual assault accusations by explaining that those women were not attractive enough for him to grope.

This is what internalized misogyny looks like. This is what deliberate, quiet-but-stubborn racism looks like.

Oh, she won the popular vote? So what. The fact is millions of Americans said one thing out loud and then indulged in hate and fear in the voting booth when no one was looking.

But now we're all looking. At the numbers. At each other. We tweet our outrage and shock, but behind all that we have fear inside of us too, now more than ever, and so we understand how this was possible.

I didn't have any classes to teach today, the day after the presidential election. I was supposed to have conferences with my students' parents for three hours this afternoon, but I couldn't.

I heard from my friends in the school building that the teachers were crying in the staff room but the students were back in class as usual, asking for bathroom breaks and extensions on papers. They thought the teachers were acting weird today.

The students at the school where I work are mostly Asian and white. We have almost no black or Latino students. We have almost no students who live near or below the poverty line and get free or reduced lunch. The median income in the school's neighborhood is almost twice that of the rest of the country.

One Asian girl in my sixth grade class's mock election explained on Monday that she would vote for Trump because his racism doesn't include Asians. She didn't mention anything about his stance on women. I thought it was funny at the time.

While my partner was at work today and my son was at school, I wanted so badly to be surrounded by a community, but I wasn't sure my school was the community I was seeking.

Maybe if I had showed up for conferences I could have found some solace. We could have grieved together as parents and teachers worried for our kids and ourselves. We could have mourned and then organized. Stronger together, Hillary Clinton said. And I still believe her.

Forget his promised immediate dismantling of the U.S. Department of Education. What will we do now that any hope for people of color, queer people, Muslim people, and women has been burned to the ground? Can we have a conference about that?

What could I have told the parents who I know would have showed up to dissect scores on their kid's recent vocabulary quizzes? How could I, in my bigly braggadocious, Humanities teacher way, pretend now that learning vocabulary even matters at all? And needing evidence and reasoning to back up a claim? And critical thinking?

There is nothing left for English teachers to defend that this election hasn't proven to be completely meaningless.

Everything I try to teach my students feels hollow now. About Bravery. About integrity. About empathy. About how the world will give back so much if we just engage with it. All my hard-fought optimism seems so ridiculous now.

Fear and hate won. Lying won. Bullying won. Last minute, I-didn't-study-I'm-just-going-to-wing-it, won. Misogyny and racism won, again.

How can any teacher be neutral now? I have no grace today.

I heard her, looking fierce and clear-faced in the color of royals, tell us that we owe him a chance to lead. I heard her reach out to our little girls. I heard her nod subtly but firmly to our right to defend our values.

But I didn't want to hear a concession speech. I wanted a rallying cry. I wanted the most qualified candidate to ever run for president of this heartbroken country to meet me at my despair and terror with rage and an action plan.

Don't go so high that you leave us now, Hillary. Please.

I don't teach again until Monday. That's a long time for my tween students. It will be complicated to talk about unreliable narrators when we come back together. Especially if I'm still crying. Or if my sadness has given way to fury by then. We will make space for conversation, either way.

That feels a little like relief. To know I'll be back in the classroom next week, surrounded by sixth graders who, whether their candidate won or lost yesterday, get it that bullies never win the long game.

Keep teaching, that's all I can do. Because even though I have very little hope for the present, my faith that our future voters will fix this mess is tremendous.

Crashing the Parties

We must fight Trump. But we must also
fight the system that delivered him to power.

by the Seattle Weekly *Editorial Board*

Now, first and foremost, we must all dig deep and find the resolve and compassion to support the women, immigrants, disabled people, people of color and others whom Donald Trump openly mocked, misrepresented, and threatened while campaigning for the presidency of the United States. It is these people who are most at risk from the policies put forth by the new president and the Republicans in control of the legislative branch of the federal government. These people deserve to be treated with dignity and respect and afforded the same path toward prosperity that has been granted white men since the founding of this country. Let there be no mistake; under a Trump presidency, their fortunes diminish—to say the very least.

We have a tremendous amount of work to do, especially the white men of this country—a demographic that voted overwhelmingly for Trump, and one that makes up a strong majority of this editorial board. We must listen to our neighbors with open minds. And we must defend those neighbors from injustice. And we must educate others like us, those who for whatever reason voted for this demagogue, in the fact that there is a better way forward. Under a Trump presidency, it is our job. This is what we must do.

But we must do even more. The forces that made Trump possible, after all, are myriad. There is a great amount of work to be done to rectify them all and revive our democracy. This is just a single suggestion.

Some have said that the presidential election of 2016 was the most important of our lifetimes. Pundits say that every four or eight years, but in this case it does appear to be true. But if that was the most important election, then we must now be in the midst of the most important post-election period of our lifetimes as well. It will require of us Americans a resolve to act, as well as a kind of clever thinking that goes beyond opposing the impending Trump presidency. For the forces that threaten our democracy are bigger than a single man.

Before looking forward, it is helpful to look back on an election season that was like no other of recent memory—though its contours were somewhat familiar, predictable even. Led by that bigoted braggart on the Republican side, he with few policy positions and a scant knowledge of the history and the workings of our federal government, the debate was a grudge match. Clinton was the vastly more appropriate, educated, and prepared candidate, with a deep working knowledge of Washington, D.C., and innumerable policy positions and plans to bring those policies to fruition. But even she was not above the fray, her sales pitch to voters in the closing weeks playing on the electorate's fears and consisting largely of tearing Trump down.

It was a degrading election based on personal attacks at a time when our country needed to have a real debate on a number of issues: trade, climate change, LGBT rights, poverty, guns, deficits, drugs, institutional racism, and infrastructure in particular. And yet so little was said about these things. In fact, a report from media watchdog Andrew Tyndall indicated that, as of October 25—just two weeks before election day—the evening newscasts of the three major broadcast networks devoted a total of 32 minutes to issues coverage *this year*—most of that pertaining to terrorism. In 2012, that number was 112. In 2008, 220. That the media is complicit in this erosion is not in doubt. Yet we believe a larger mechanism is at play here, one that we the people must combat.

It is no secret that the two people who took the stage for the first presidential debate on September 26 were the two most unpopular candidates in our lifetimes. According to a recent ABC/Post poll, 60 percent of respondents viewed Donald Trump unfavorably, while 56 percent viewed Clinton unfavorably.

A significant amount of Clinton's troubles with the populace can be traced back to a set of "scandals" manufactured by congressional Republicans who have been campaigning against Clinton for the past four years—if not the past 25. Surely another dose of unpopularity comes from the fact that she's a woman in a country where gender still determines how much you are valued in the workplace. Trump's unpopularity was more honestly won. At a fundamental level, his campaign was built on binaries: us vs. Mexicans, us vs. Muslims, us vs. the cucks. Naturally, such othering is going to appeal only to a particular segment of our shrinking white populace while disgusting and frightening the rest of us.

Yet the displeasure with these candidates goes beyond them as individuals and can be traced back to recent history. The fact is that in 2008, two events caused rifts within our electorate—at first seemingly fleeting, but since proven undeniable.

One was the election of the first black president, a collective act that we here at *Seattle Weekly* celebrated and still view as a great credit to our country. But for a significant portion of the population, Barack Obama's election was viewed as a threat, at first described as encroaching socialism by the emergent Tea Party and spoken of in a thinly veiled racism that cast the president as something un-American—a racism given its greatest endorsement by Donald Trump, who essentially launched his presidential bid as the standard-bearer of the Birther movement. Trump's candidacy, unvarnished by decency, has pulled the veil away and led to a newly emboldened white-nationalist movement.

The other event was the sub-prime mortgage crisis, which sent the economy into a tailspin in the waning days of the George W. Bush administration. President Obama righted the ship and set the American economy on the long road to incremental recovery that has us now on firmer footing. But the gains have not been equally distributed; the gap between rich and poor is as large as it has been since the Great Depression, and the bankers responsible for the collapse were never penalized for their careless, greedy actions. The result was the Occupy movement of 2011, which emerged at the same time as the Tea Party was gaining political power.

Both these nascent movements found a new maturity in the race for the White House that began in earnest in 2015. On the right, the new nationalists found a hero in Trump and pushed him to an improbable victory in the Republican primary. On the left, it was Vermont Senator Bernie Sanders who captured the populist passions of progressives who viewed Clinton as a continuation of the less appealing aspects of the Obama and Bill Clinton presidencies, her hawkish foreign-policy stances and coziness with Wall Street at odds with their ideals. Unlike Trump, Sanders was unable to surmount the machinery of his chosen party and, with the help of superdelegates and favoritism from party leadership, Clinton prevailed.

Meanwhile, Republican leaders were putting some distance between themselves and Trump's rhetoric, the bravest among them speaking out against the candidate and, in some cases, endorsing Clinton. The cowards gave lip service to decency while pulling the lever for the know-nothing bigot. Progressive voters protested Clinton's candidacy in the general, even as she reshaped her policy positions to adhere more closely to Sanders' platform. Calls to keep the Sanders movement going were hectored by those, including Sanders himself, who viewed a Trump presidency as too great a threat to risk a loss at the hands of a split party. Indeed, once the conventions were over, few on the left dared criticize Clinton for fear of empowering Trump. There were other options on many state ballots—the libertarian Gary Johnson and Green Party candidate Jill Stein—but the danger was too great.

Now that the voting is long since over, it is time to get real. No matter the outcome—even if Trump would have lost by a landslide and crawled back into the gilded rathole from which he came—what this election laid bare is the disservice the two-party system does to all of us. Just as many liberals were holding their tongues against Hillary, many Republicans who had once vowed never to support Trump got in league with unapologetic racists and misogynists for fear that Clinton would be president. Of course, voters always have to make some calculation in the ballot box; no candidate can be the perfect choice for everyone. Yet the fact remains that 2016 proved we need more viable options.

This election presents an opportunity—and, frankly, an obligation—to tweak the great democratic experiment that began so many years ago. We must adjust the current system and find ways to make third- (and fourth- and fifth-) party politics possible and not just a disruptive sideshow. We need to present a way for conservatives who did not identify with Trump's extremist views, but felt compelled to vote for him anyway for lack of a better option, a party of their own. We need a party for Sanders supporters that is more robust than "Not Trump." Under such a system, Clinton could have been a more trustworthy candidate, because she would have been free to argue for the centrist Democratic government she represents, without all the awkward appendages slapped on to appease her party's far left. Many Americans remain believers in free trade. Why shouldn't they have a proven supporter of such policies at the podium making the case?

A common argument against plurality democracy is that among the multitudes of parties that result, some espouse extreme nationalist rhetoric—such as we are seeing in nearly every European democracy today. Yet our two-party system let Trump through. It allowed him to become president as the outspoken racists in our country cheered. Whatever bulwark against such a xenophobic and sexist demagogue we thought we had is not working. In such an environment, it would be preferable to have a white-nationalist party in America that could provide an exit ramp to the deplorables—we said it!—who are supporting Trump as an explicit expression of white supremacy. With only two parties to choose from, the most hateful, bigoted parts of the voting populace get folded into either one or the other. There is nowhere else for them to go. And when an outspoken brute like Trump comes along, the whole party is tarred with the same brush. When they feel they have no other option, as cowardly as that stance may be, they might even elect him.

And, even supposing Clinton had won, what would have happened to Trump's supporters? Is it better that the Republican party squash them with a mechanism like the Democrats' superdelegates so they feel they have no political recourse? Without such recourse, violence becomes a more likely option. A third party would allow a release valve for racism and hatred that cannot be ignored and threatens to explode if contained.

The bottom line is this: No matter who would have won the presidential election, the majority of Americans—those who voted for the loser combined with those who reluctantly voted for the victor—would not be satisfied with their new president. And we call this democracy?

There are many reasons we have never been able to break out of this system, but the main one has been that the national conversation about third parties largely stops after each presidential election. Which is why we are raising the point now. Yes we must attempt to avert disaster in the immediate term, and later to regain what was lost, but we also must establish ways to make sure it never happens again.

Parties, as Madison tells us in *The Federalist Papers*, are inevitable in a democracy. Coalitions are advantageous, and so naturally form. But the two-party system is very much a result of specific choices we've made as a society. Some of this stems from the arbitrary barriers states erect to limit third-party access to the ballot. Washington state has rightly begun to break these down, both through the low threshold for signatures required for candidates to appear on the presidential ballots and the top-two primary system for all other offices that saps power from the two major parties. And yet these measures hardly fix the systemic issues at hand.

Most political scientists agree that the reason the United States is locked into a two-party system is that the vast majority of our elections are winner-take-all: As long as you get more votes than the next person, you get 100 percent of the spoils. This makes a third-party candidacy almost certainly a non-starter, since any third-party candidate will inevitably leach more votes from one major-party candidate than the other, creating a situation in which voting for your ideals (Nader) helps elect the antithesis to your ideals (Bush). In a winner-take-all system, it is inevitable that two factions will arise, since getting 50.1 percent of the vote is the surest way to victory.

A number of electoral systems have been designed to avoid this conundrum.

One is a system called "ranked-choice voting," in which voters rank their preference for candidates. Whichever candidate gets the least number of top rankings is eliminated, and voters who named them their first choice see their votes assigned to their second choice; the process repeats until a candidate gets 50 percent of the vote. It's still winner-take-all, but it reduces the penalty voters pay for voting for third-party candidates. Also, it might allow parties to more easily reach the thresholds for inclusion in public financing and debates. This alone would be a great service to the country, as it would allow a broader spectrum of ideas into the national conversation.

A more drastic step would be to convert the federal government to a parliamentary system in which parties are assigned government power based on the proportion of the vote they get. Yet that would require a constitutional overhaul that, even in this conversation of drastic change, may prove too drastic in the near term.

In most states, ranked voting would require approval by legislatures that are controlled by members of the parties who derive great power from the status quo. Then again, voters in Maine just approved a referendum to create this very system. In Washington state, as noted above, we have already proven ourselves willing to experiment with the way we choose our candidates. We should double down on that spirit now and adopt ranked voting—as a start. This will not immediately solve our problems, but by setting an early example, Washington state could help begin the march toward a more representative democracy.

The daunting nature of the challenge should not be a deterrent. Ask yourselves: How many more elections like this year's can our country endure? We are a nation of coal miners choosing between the party that would close the mine and the party that aids and abets executives who literally put the workers' lives at risk through lax safety regulations; gay business owners choosing between a party that would increase regulations on their enterprise and a party that derives power from denigrating the way they feel love; pacifists choosing between a candidate who's had a hand in every American armed conflict for the past 20 years and a candidate who would do away with nuclear nonproliferation; Occupiers deciding between a New York millionaire and a New York billionaire (or so he says).

We have convinced ourselves that this is normal, that there is no other way. We have convinced ourselves this is representative democracy. So why don't we feel represented?

A version of this editorial was first published on November 9, 2016. At that time, the Seattle Weekly *editorial board consisted of Bob Baranski, Mark Baumgarten, Sara Bernard, Casey Jaywork, Daniel Person, and Kelton Sears.*

On Fear and Anger and Fighting Back

by Reagan Jackson

Jab, jab, straight. V dip, hook punch. I keep my feet moving and my guard up, in sync my partner. It's the 11th session of a 14-week boxing class called We Fight Back and we are finally sparring. My shirt is soaked through with sweat and my muscles are screaming, but I am grinning through my mouth guard. I've needed this.

It's been 16 years since the last time I wore a pair of boxing gloves. I was lighter then, in the best shape of my life. I am a different fighter now, more grounded and strategic. Even with less stamina, my punches knock my partner back a few steps and land with a satisfying thud.

I love sparring. The adrenalin, the sweat, the way power feels in my body. When I am fighting it's one of the few times I feel like all of me is in alignment. My mind is never clearer. But my love of fighting has always been complicated by my relationship to violence.

Throughout childhood, my dad tried to get me involved in martial arts, but I considered myself a pacifist until middle school when bullying reached a fevered pitch. Though I never started a fight, almost daily the fight found me. I stopped worrying about hurting people and started worrying about them hurting me. A boy in my class hit me with a brass edge folder slicing a gash just a quarter of an inch beneath my eye. Any higher and I would have been permanently blind. As it was, I had to get stitches. I was humiliated, but worse I was angry.

This was no casual emotion. It was a raw primal Incredible Hulk anger, what bell hooks would call a killing rage. Every time I saw that kid I wanted to smash his face in. I began to have violent fantasies, each more warped than the next. My rage became a source of shame and fear, confirmation that I was truly a terrible person. My parents were concerned. My dad kept pushing me to take karate, but I steadfastly refused because I didn't trust myself. I thought if someone taught me how to really fight I might actually kill someone.

I didn't start boxing until my senior year of college. My junior year was simultaneously the best and worst year of my life. I moved to Spain to study Spanish and fell in love with cream sherry, flamenco music and beach lounging. I also lost my best friend in a car crash and I was roofied.

I don't know what drug it was, but I still remember every moment. A stranger bought me a drink. I was perpetually at a party those days, so it was a pretty common occurrence. But almost as soon as I drank it I knew something was wrong. I tried to convince my friends to take me home. They didn't want to leave the bar, so they put me in a cab.

By the time I got to my apartment building the drug had taken hold and I was completely immobilized. The cab driver had to carry me out of the car. He took me to the entrance of my apartment building and laid me across the marble steps. First, he paid himself by taking all the money from my pocket, then he reached inside my shirt. My whole body was frozen, but I was lucid. I couldn't move, but I could scream and did. This was sufficient to scare him away, but then I lay there alone in the middle of the night on the streets of a foreign country feeling terrified and praying no one else would find me. I don't know how long it took before the drug wore off and I was able to feel my arms and legs again, but it felt like hours. I know I am lucky and that it could have been so much worse. Still, I had never felt so powerless in my life.

The rage I had been so careful to suppress rose up in me larger than ever and it would not go away. I was mad at my friends for abandoning me the one time I needed them. I was mad at myself for being reckless, mad at God for taking my best friend, and mad at every person, place or situation that had ever made me feel powerless. It was the kind of fury that burns you from the inside out like acid. I had to find somewhere to put it. So I started boxing.

After a year of boxing, I got the opportunity to move to Japan. I traded fighting for meditating. I didn't fight again for several years when I took up taekwondo. I received my black belt in 2010 shortly before another travel opportunity took me away from my training. Getting my black belt was what cured me of fearing my own power. With skill came discipline and being in control of my own body gave me the peace I had been searching for.

I have endured an entire lifetime of people fucking with me. Even now I feel like I am constantly fighting to assert my humanity, to be allowed to live in this world. I think that's why boxing feels so satisfying because for one hour a week when I feel the world pummeling me I can finally punch back. I can take all the rage and sadness and righteous indignation, shove it into my fists and punch until my arms are sore and I can't breathe.

Now trapped in the waking nightmare of having a president-elect endorsed by the KKK, the fight has only begun. We have elected a bully who has effectively normalized openly racist, Islamaphobic, and misogynist behavior. Hate crimes are already on the rise and it's no surprise when I turn on the news and our nation's "leader" is up on rape charges and caught on video unapologetically laughing about how he assaults women.

"So much of my life work has been around stopping male violence against women and challenging gender-based violence that I'm just so sick of women being raped and murdered and brutalized and beaten," confessed Ane Mathieson when asked what inspired the creation of We Fight Back.

Mathieson and Megan Murphy, both social workers, teamed up about two and half years ago to pilot the first class. "I wanted to create an opportunity for women to fight and defend themselves from violence, but I wanted them to be able to do that for free," said Mathieson. "So I reached out to a friend of mine who is an MMA instructor."

MMA stands for Mixed Martial Arts. The first project involved eight women including Murphy and Mathieson. In addition to learning physical skills for self-defense, they hosted concurrent conversations about gender-based violence. "So that's been a big challenge," said Mathieson. "Creating a space where women can feel comfortable to start really talking about this stuff authentically but then not feeling like that means that can't have relationships with men or that it means that they have to hate every man."

After the first program, Murphy and Mathieson took stock of what went well and what needed to change. "The first cohort we had was all white women and we all knew that this was not okay," said Mathieson. While the program is open to all women, Murphy and Mathieson wanted to make sure it addressed the fact that women of color and queer identified women are disproportionately impacted by violence.

Another challenge was having a male identified instructor. This was a trigger for participants who had been assaulted by men, but neither Murphy nor Mathieson had previous experience with fighting. They decided to bring Genevieve Corrin as a third partner because of her experience with boxing and this paved the way for a new partnership with Cappy's Gym. Located in the Central District, Cappy's gym has been making boxing accessible for everyone since 1999.

The women in my cohort are a diverse mix of 20 and 30 somethings, some first-time fighters and some, like me, returning after a long break. There is a camaraderie that has grown between us over the past months. All of us have our own personal relationship to violence and fighting, some with more trauma than others, but despite the different motivations our goal is the same, to prepare ourselves for the inevitability of a fight.

For 20-year-old Azeb Tuji, We Fight Back was just something that sounded cool. "It just sounded so out of my comfort zone and something that I wouldn't be able to do and something like so kick ass that I was like yeah I need to do something like that for myself."

Tuji, a first-time fighter, recounts that the only physical fights she's been in have been with her brothers when she was a kid, but she is not new to confrontation. "I think the last couple of weeks I've been getting harassed and people are trying to talk to me more," said Tuji. "But instead of kind of lowering my voice or something or being like 'ok' I've been getting super angry and my fist are clenched and I'm just ready to go."

After an hour of physical training there is a short break, then boxers trade gloves for pens and notepads and reconvene for an hour of curriculum facilitated by Murphy and Mathieson. Often we begin with a meditation or a centering, a reminder that we are more than just bodies fighting, that we are minds, hearts and spirits too. Sometimes there are experiential activities that get us on our feet and in our voices. And always there are robust conversations.

"I'm the person that comes up with the drills and the focus and themes behind each class every week," says boxing coach Olivia Mendez. "Prior to the start of any of the classes, we all sat and thought about the components. Number one: who are we working with and what do they want to know?"

Mendez began boxing 15 years ago after a bad breakup left her searching for an outlet for pent up emotions. "I think one of the canons that We Fight Back speaks to is that myself as a woman growing up when and where I did, I didn't have a lot of opportunities to experience my emotions," says Mendez. "I really struggled with how to cope with that confrontation."

This seems to be a common refrain. What do you do when conflict occurs? In our last class, Mendez described the three most common gut reactions. Fight, flight or freeze.

We separated into three groups based on our default reactions then we boxed a round operating from that paradigm. After years of running away from my anger and trying to avoid conflict, I've finally succumbed to my base reflex, to fight. The first round I gave no quarter. I used my size to force my partner to back up, but then the next round Coach Mendez asked us to practice using a different response.

For three minutes I had to freeze instead of punching. It's one thing to take a punch and then return fire and a totally different feeling to just stand there. Though running away isn't my default either, when I practiced boxing on the defensive it at least gave me a sense that I was doing something, blocking and ducking, but just standing there frozen I felt like a victim.

For Tuji, We Fight Back has given her the confidence to unfreeze. When she's confronted with microaggressions from her coworkers, she has begun to speak up. "Even though it's like hardly saying it, I'm learning how to stand up for myself," she says.

For some like Mathieson, whose default is to attack, there is a realization that being reactionary is still no guarantee of safety. "I'm really mouthy and when men harass me on the streets I have a whole slew of tactics that I have to respond to them and I sometimes am really aggressive," she said. "There have been so many times where I'm like 'I am going to get my face bashed in'. One of these days one of these men is going to bash my face in and I really want to know how to defend myself in case that happens."

While it's been good to get back into my body, to engage with an incredible community of women and to experience the release that fighting provides, participating in We Fight Back has also brought to the surface a deep-seated grief. I'm tired of always having to fight back, of being told not to walk at night, or being made to feel as though my basic human rights are privileges.

This war I'm fighting in is not against men or white people, but against the white supremacist, heteronormative patriarchy which has done everything in its power to create, sustain and normalize bullying and rape culture. We live in an environment where we learn early on that our bodies are not our own, that we should expect to be judged by how we choose to dress or how willing we are to be complicit in our own victimization. It's exhausting and it's not just happening here, it's happening all over the world.

More than a class, a community or even free boxing lessons, We Fight Back is a declaration that women are ready to stand in their power. That's what keeps me coming back week after week, knowing that I am not only contributing to my own strength and self-empowerment but that I am part of a broader movement demanding justice in my community.

Why You Voted the Way You Did

by Hanna Brooks Olsen

In the month leading up to The Incident, my phone was warm to the touch; between my own compulsive checking of polls and data and the messages flooding in from every possible platform, that poor device spent late summer and fall working overtime.

What do you make of this race? What's this candidate like? Where should I phone-bank? Where should I donate money?

So many people I knew—and some I didn't, really—were searching for answers about that big ballot. I tried to do my best to answer truthfully and with nuance.

As the last drops came in that Tuesday, the questions didn't stop, but they did change.

Is this real? Can you believe it? And of course, *What do I do?*

Even a month after the election, I still heard that last question every single day.

Maybe you experienced the same thing—maybe you're the political friend, the comforting friend, the friend that serves as a touchstone for the people around you. Or maybe you were the one tossing out lifelines, looking for a light in the darkness.

I have become convinced that most of us fall into one of two camps; there are the people who are, as my friend eloquently put it in the days after the election, anointed with the "sacred trust," and there are the people who look to these sources. Or perhaps we all play both roles depending on the situation.

In the lead-up to the election, I was selected to be the Scholar in Residence at Town Hall in Seattle. From this station, I learned several things. One is that it is becoming increasingly more difficult to find local community programming and journalism that directly addresses local politics and, specifically, down-ballot races that does not come directly from campaigns. Another is that, in this era of fake news and Facebook echo chambers, people want—and, I'd argue, need—those programs and outlets more than ever.

But one of the biggest lessons I've learned is that unless we personally prepare and educate ourselves, we are set up to fail when it comes to determining who to trust and how to vote—in large part because we don't know where to turn to help us form our opinions and cast our ballots.

Voting is important and holy and necessary and righteous, but it's also tedious and time-consuming and tiresome and sometimes it is downright fucking boring.

We vote on the things that impact us but we also vote on the things that will impact people for generations. We vote on things that are so much bigger than we are. We vote for people we've never met and will never meet and can't possibly know. And we do it based on a combination of second-hand information—what we can glean from dry voter guides, the news, and what we learn through the game of telephone that is social media.

When you pause for a moment and think about how much is tied up in a vote—how much it means to vote, how much trust is placed in the electorate—it should be apparent that there is a voracious appetite for answers. However, thanks to our human brains and survival instincts, we are hardwired to look for answers that are primarily validating, comforting, reassuring, and then, possibly, as a byproduct, informative.

Unfortunately, we don't know what we don't know and, sometimes, we're not sure we know what we think we know. Which makes it hard when our ballots come in the mail and we have to dig deep and find an opinion about every issue and person.

I found in my Town Hall research that, to make sense of it all, we are turning less to trusted news sources and more to trusted people and personalities.

As much as we wring our hands about our personal feedback loops, it seems to me that they are less constructed of outlets we trust and more a framework or web of people, or at least, personalities.

We all like to think of ourselves as smart—a YouGov poll found that 55 percent of respondents believe they're smarter than the average American—and we especially like it when *other* people think we're smart. Which means we're more likely to trust people, information, and sources which make us feel and seem smart. And nothing makes you feel and seem more smart than selectively choosing to listen to voices that match the ideas you already possess.

But what is it that defines those people? Whose job is it to be those people and how can we ensure that they are—that we are—providing information that is, quite literally, trustworthy?

For starters, I think it's impossible to talk about trust and voting and the media without talking about money. It is abundantly clear that funding is a major issue in journalism; journalists face layoffs constantly and newsrooms have been thinned out to a point of near extinction. It's also an unfortunate reality that campaign season is what keeps many news stations on the air. Wealthy donors have a vested interest in keeping the coffers of PACs full and the commercial breaks of your favorite singing competition choked with hit pieces.

These are not unrelated circumstances.

There is, indeed, exponentially more money being pumped into messaging and coercing the story than there is in reporting what is actually occurring—but the problem is not just that so-called objective journalism has been silently, slowly asphyxiated by PACs.

It's also that we, as consumers, have not been clear in our own desires or expectations.

It can't be overstated that the media does not drive itself. We drive the media that we see. If you have ever snarked at someone for sharing a Kardashian-related story on Facebook (to yourself or, perhaps more sanctimoniously, in the comments) only to go ahead and click through and read the entire thing, you've all but ensured that more Kardashian news will not only be produced and set free into the world, but that more of it will show up in your Facebook feed, because you've told both the purveyor of the story and Facebook itself that you do, in fact, enjoy Kardashian updates.

Clicks are also the driver behind the epidemic of fake news; one purveyor of fake news confirmed to NPR that it was not uncommon to make five figures per month

from the ads that accompany such stories. He wouldn't give exact figures, but he said news stories about other fake-news proprietors making between $10,000 and $30,000 a month apply to him.

News creators—whether fake or otherwise—know their audience, they know how to drive traffic, and, they know how to stay afloat financially. You may not like the content, but if you're clicking on it, you're telling them to keep making it because it'll keep the lights on.

This is true of legacy outlets, it's true of newcomers, it's true of local blogs with ads, and it's true of sites that exist solely to spread incorrect information for a profit.

If you exist in a mostly lefty world, like I do, you may not have been exposed to the worst of the fake news wave that resulted in so many real news headlines—and that's because of who clicks it and who shares it (and there's also the not-insignificant fact that many fake news sites are run out of Russia).

The arbiters of fake news have admitted that they gain much more ground with conservative angles, telling an NPR reporter that liberals simply don't take the bait as often. Pro-Trump articles seem to receive higher engagement rates—more comments, shares, and likes—which drives their visibility. An independent analysis from Buzzfeed found that while the most-shared real news stories of the 2016 election cycle were largely in favor of Hillary Clinton or, at least, against Donald

Trump, the most viral fake news stories were nearly all—except for one—against the democratic nominee.

However, lefties like me ought not get too smug. We're also guilty of looking for content which confirms our biases. Another independent analysis found that the Facebook pages of popular liberal-leaning websites were often spreading factually inaccurate information.

The investigation found that while 94 percent of CNN's posts to Facebook were considered "mostly true," just 49 percent of the news from Occupy Democrats was. Close to 18 percent of the Facebook posts from Addicting Info were a mix of true and false. On the Facebook page for The Other 98%, the posts which netted the highest engagement were those which were completely untrue. Overall, close to 20 percent of the content posted to left-leaning Facebook pages was either completely false or a mix of true and false.

The analysis looked only at the Facebook posts by pages and not the content that those posts linked to. At a glance, this may seem like an incomplete dataset—was the news article itself incorrect or false, or just the headline? Turns out, it doesn't matter; an estimated six in 10 social media users will share a link without reading the article, meaning that the only information they *have* is what's in the headline.

Conventional news is also, of course, not without its flaws. Arguably, the coverage of the 2016 election by mainstream media sites was just as detrimental to the pursuit of information. The normalization of Donald Trump, the continued bias against Black and brown people, the breathless coverage of live events without all the information, and the unwillingness to fact-check guests who actively spew racism and misogyny are part of the reason why Americans are looking for new ways to get news.

Largely, they seem to be looking to social media—though they seem dubious of that, as well. A Pew study from this year found that 66 percent of people say they get their news from Facebook. But just 12 percent say they trust the news they find there.

Then again, only 32 percent say they trust the media at *all*.

Though, if you believe *Breitbart*, a "news" website that has actively sought to undermine the mainstream news at every turn, you'd see reporting that less than 6 percent of people trust the media.

That figure is incorrect, and it is indicative of a broader problem—the epidemic of hyper-partisan websites and misinformation campaigns have sought to both convince the masses of things that are untrue while also undermining the collective trust we put in media, generally.

It's a one-two punch to democracy and to literacy and it's one that has consequences.

The epidemic of hyper-partisan, sensationalist, and fake news (as well as the inclination to share without reading) is, in part, due to the money that stands to be made—the owners of those viral Facebook pages can easily charge thousands for one post, due to their huge audiences—but it's also down to our own response to it. Which, I think, can be linked to oversaturation.

We, as a species, want to be in the know—which means that often we are trying to scoop up information on a lot of things at once from wherever we can get them. But between our myriad social media feeds, the email newsletters, and the constant churning of TV news, there's so much material flying at us on a given day that it is difficult for a lot of us to pause and be critical of the source.

So we trust what sounds right, or what comes from someone we know (or think) to be trustworthy. We trust our friends and family, we believe they are smart people—so surely, the things they share or engage with online *must* be trustworthy, right?

The human brain tends to place a great deal of trust in people and personalities, rather than actual knowledge. A 2012 study conducted by Microsoft and Carnegie Mellon found that a Tweet from a person you like or trust is more likely to lend credibility to a story you see on Twitter than the author's demonstrated expertise.

Users are poor judges of truthfulness based on content alone, and instead are influenced by heuristics such as user name when making credibility assessments

Determinations of trustworthiness are also hopelessly bound up in physical appearance and attraction; a 2014 New York University study found that we decide if a person can be trusted or not within milliseconds, and that much of that trust is bound up in how conventionally attractive they are—high cheekbones, for example, make a person seem more trustworthy.

A litany of sexist jokes aside, the fact is that Fox News and its use of conventionally-attractive blonde women is actually incredibly clever from a sociological standpoint (particularly considering we tend to trust women slightly more, though not about their own experiences). This is also why you trust people on Twitter who have more attractive photos, and even news stories with stock images featuring better-looking people.

In short: What we say is "I don't trust the media" or "I don't trust news I get on Facebook," but what we demonstrate is that we do trust *some* media and we *definitely* trust media that's shared by our friends or personalities we like.

In a great many ways, we're also wired to seek out echo chambers, as much as we may shun the idea of them verbally. It's why we tend to vote for candidates who confirm our beliefs about the world.

The human brain is conditioned to listen for information. At a neurological level, we just really like to hear other people—especially people we like or trust—talking about issues we care about, particularly when they echo our own beliefs. Research published in 2009 found that when your brain hears a good story, one that it can empathize with, it releases a burst of oxytocin. A story or a particularly engrossing conversation or article can also put more of the brain to work, which makes it more interesting.

This is why your voter's guide is so ruthlessly boring, but a panel discussion is, at least, slightly less so. This is also why we're drawn to magnanimous candidates like Barack Obama, but less wowed by more low-key orators.

Tuning things out that you don't like or want to hear is actually a survival mechanism; your brain tries to conserve resources by not releasing oxytocin, which means it prizes information that seems important. And it's much easier to find information important when it plays well with your existing neural pathways—the reason metaphors work so well is because they help your brain draw connections.

Additionally, your brain responds well and with pleasure when—and here's something that will not surprise many people—*you're* the subject of a conversation. Information that conflicts with your worldview is decidedly not about you, does not center you, and does not validate your existence—so you're more likely to dislike it, because it's not creating a joy or pleasure response.

When Donald Trump says America isn't great, the brains of people who feel that it isn't great are engaged. When he stokes the flames of xenophobia, it confirms the existing fears of voters. It doesn't matter that he offers few other trust indicators—his platform, in many ways, speaks directly to the needs of the brains of his supporters.

This is also why the idea of "identity politics" is not only dismissive of large portions of the population, it also ignores the science; voters trust people who look like them, sure, but more than that, they vote for candidates who speak to their lived experience. When you can see your experience in a candidate or issues, you're more likely to feel positively toward that candidate or issue and, as such, build trust.

This is also why I think we turn to actual humans, having actual conversations. Or, at least, actual humans having digital conversations. This explains the draw toward TV news and it explains the demand for local programming.

In local elections, issues of trustworthiness are slightly mitigated; instead of relying on sensational national news, it's easy to host debates and write editorials which contain primary information from people we personally know and trust.

I know talking politics is taboo but it became clear to me in my time at Town Hall that people really, really just want to talk and listen to others talk about local elections. If you've ever attended a panel where the Q&A devolved into a series of people giving their own opinions in the form of a question, you know that there is a deep desire for conversation and to be listened to.

This helps us sort out where to direct our caring, as well.

When everything is all-caps important, when it's all flooding in so quickly, it's incredibly difficult to determine the hierarchy of importance. Our time, attention, and resources are all finite. And honestly, it's just easier a lot of the time to delegate some of the thinking to someone else. Someone we trust.

Yes, our vote is our sacred bond with democracy but good lord, have you seen how many things we're expected to be somewhat of an expert on?

And I think that explains a lot of what we seek out, whether it's a panel, a conversation among friends, or a direct connection over text or Facebook Messenger. Sometimes we just need someone else to help us make sense of the complicated parts of the law and politics.

So that leaves us with that question: What do we do?

How do we, as voters, know where to place our trust? What do we do now and how do we ensure that the electorate is making its decisions—which is to say, instilling its trust—in the people and campaigns that will result in the most good for the most people? Because of course, that's why we vote. We vote to influence the future. We vote to have our say in the collective next steps.

To start, we must expect more of our local service providers and give them the tools to do it. Whether it's nonprofits, tech innovators, or media, I believe we've allowed, by voting with our clicks and our dollars, the vacuum of media space to be taken up by untrustworthy sources. It's time to invest in the organizations and systems that we love—including democracy itself, and media as an extension.

This year, Southern California radio station KPCC created a Human Voter Guide program that included a hotline and call-in shows where people could directly ask their questions to a trusted source. This is what media outlets can do when they're supported and they know people want it. Which I think they do.

We used to have something like that; For six years, the City of Seattle was blessed with the citizen-powered Living Voters Guide, a joint service of the University of Washington and CityClub, which provided fact-checking from the city's public libraries. It was a valuable, information-rich resource, but it was discontinued in 2016. I think the election cycle might have been different without it, at least locally.

But donating to public media and attending events and voting with your clicks and dollars may still not feel concrete enough. I suspect that's why, on election night and beyond, I've received so many messages asking, simply: What can I do? Where do I go?

My answer has been—and remains—the following:

Find one thing to really care about. Then find a provider or an organization who focuses on that. Give them your time and energy and attention and money. Do it because warm bodies at the doors can make a huge difference, but do it, too, because it's a public service to create an army of well-informed voters who can use their trust capital to combat false information.

Dedicate to one thing and become the expert on that thing in your circle. Be the trusted friend on that issue. In doing this, you become an essential part of our web of information in the city and in your online spheres. In the last few months, it's become increasingly clear to me that this is essential. Attend panels. Volunteer. Read articles.

If you feel like you can't trust anyone, it's essential to become trustworthy yourself.

It's not enough to simply mourn the death of the media or services or to wring our hands. We can only yell about fake news so much before we have to provide something real to replace it. We vote every year, several times each year, and we need to be prepared with information when we can. Much as we have put our trust into each other, we have to put our trust into providers and systems—or, maybe, we have to begin building that trust ourselves.

Being an Activist Parent Post-Election

by Sharon H. Chang

On election day I had every intention of getting my 7-year-old to bed on time. But we stayed up late glued to the TV. It felt critical. Eventually he passed out exhausted on the futon while my husband and I continued to stare horrified at the screen. After our worst fears were confirmed, my husband carried our boy downstairs and laid him in bed.

On Wednesday my son awoke and asked immediately, "Who won?" When he heard the result his face fell. "Did all the Muslims get kicked out of the country?" "No," I assured him, "It's okay for now." He asked how long Trump would be President and I told him four years. "That means I'll be eleven years old when Trump kills me." I was shocked. "Whoa whoa whoa! Trump isn't going to kill you. You're going to be fine." He looked back at me a little shamefaced, "But I feel like he's going to kill me."

On Thursday I needed community. I was experiencing the worst insomnia of my adult life and knew my fears and anxieties were running deep. Got Green was holding a post-election conversation for mourning, healing, and to talk about impacts upon communities of color. Of course I was going. At the conversation I stayed upstairs with the grownups. My son went downstairs to childcare. I didn't have time to feed him. He didn't like the food at the event and ended up eating potato chips and chocolate for dinner.

On Friday I needed to get active. I helped organize a family/child-centered post-election dialogue in collaboration with Families of Color Seattle. We drew monsters to help children outlet their feelings and superheroes to tap into their power and strength. I sketched a flaming monster and myself sitting small and sad next to it. My son's monster looked like a tiny blue octopus. "Look mom! I made a germ. And I'm going to draw myself big so I don't have to look at it."

That night I was photographer for a Women and Trans People of Color Healing Cipher; part of a national #our100 movement to bring forward the voices of survivors of color in response to the gendered violence of Trump's campaign. It was a small sacred space and I didn't want my son interrupting while people were grieving together. So I sat him in a corner with the iPad and he played games by himself for hours.

On Saturday at home there were no groceries, laundry wasn't done, the house was filthier than it had been in months. I still wasn't sleeping. I was ragged, on-edge, raw. I went to an equity training for work where (of course) we talked about the election. My son went to childcare. Again. When I picked him up he was so hungry he cried. I gave him a bagel and grapes I'd grabbed at the training.

On Monday I got a press release that Seattle students were walking out in protest. Even though Monday is our family day, I had a gut feeling I needed to get out there too and photograph. My husband picked up our son at school while I was marching. When I was done the two of them came to get me. But I was tired and distracted. Later that evening my best friend, who is trans and part of our chosen family, was verbally assaulted by transphobic men. They cited Trump's presidency as license for their violence.

One week post-election (the following Wednesday) we were driving home from school when my son solemnly said, "Mom, do you like me?" "What do you mean??," I exclaimed. "I *love* you! Why do you ask me that?" "Because," he answered frankly, "you never play with me." He whimpered sleeping that night; had a nightmare about cavemen; woke at 2:30am; went back to sleep; had another nightmare about giants; woke again and couldn't go back to sleep.

My heart fell a million miles and shattered into pieces on the ground.

Tonight we were supposed to go to the Youth Speaks Seattle Poetry Slam Series kickoff with my best friend. I couldn't do it. Instead I texted my friend what had happened and that I felt like a shit-awful mother. They instantly wrote back, "You're not a shit-awful mom! Shit is fucking complicated right now. We are all doing the best we can."

For sure. These last weeks have been terrifying for so many of us in similar and different ways. The Southern Poverty Law Center has collected more than 400 (now 700) reports of hateful intimidation and harassment since the election.

The vast majorityof these post-election hate incidents have been anti-immigrant and anti-Black and have occurred at K-12 schools and universities. That report alone would be enough to send any parent into a tailspin. And certainly the question "What do we tell our children?" has loomed incredibly large since fateful election night as epitomized beautifully by Van Jones' impassioned CNN commentary. I have seen a maybe an unprecedented but telling increase to reach out to families with resources, support, space for how to deal with bigotry.

As hate rises and the President-Elect continues to announce alarming appointment after appointment including climate change deniers, far-right figures and nationalists (earning wide praise from white supremacists and neo-Nazis)—it is absolutely right and important to feel worried, scared, scattered and energized to fight.

But as you can see the formula for family resistance is, well, complicated.

Certainly my son is frightened and wants equity as much as me. But I can skip meals if I need to get something done. As a growing young person, he can't. I can have sleepless nights and say "oh it's insomnia." But he can't. I need to talk, and talk, and talk about it some more. He can talk some but then needs to talk about other things like stories, jokes, Pokemon cards and Minecraft. I need to organize. He needs to play. *With me.* Simply put, he needs me to take care of him to be strong in his resistance.

It all begs super important questions about how we sustain being active and political when we are caregivers. Not only are there many forces encouraging depoliticization of families in this racist, sexist, classist, xeno-, islama-, trans-, and homophobic country, but that push to depoliticize is compounded enormously when there's meals to be made, cleaning to do, errands to run and so much to lose if the caring of our loved ones falls to the wayside.

I am an author, scholar and activist. Understandably I kicked into hyper overdrive post-election as many activists have. It's a lot. Still I'm proud of and honored to do the work I do. I feel an urgency to do it now of course more than ever and plan to propel forward. I'm also the mother of a young child and partner to a husband who works long self-employed hours. I keep moving by taking my son with me to a lot of things. I have always believed firmly that it was good for him. That remains true. We've had incredible conversations before, during and post-election.

Yet it can and does take a toll. While every working mother feels the heart-pull of work versus family, the context of my political efforts are very specific. Especially now. I still lie awake middle of the night and worriedly scroll my Facebook feed to see what new awful appointments have been made, what actions are being planned, how people are doing. It's easy to get overwhelmed, fatigued, spread thin, short-tempered. At the same time there's the conviction to keep going hard because the stakes are so high. So where is the solution to this seemingly impossible equation?

In the end it's been my 7-year-old son who has had sage wisdom to give to me. Yes it's crucial to get out there. However balance matters. Sometimes staying home and re-energizing is the revolution. It's important to care but it's important to care for ourselves too. That, I think, must be the key to plugging in and sustaining. Being a politicized family (whatever that family looks like) means we daily work to make change *and*—no matter what's going on in the world—we simultaneously work to be together, break bread, and have fun whenever and wherever we can. With our love for each other nourished solid in place—I suspect we can never be broken. As my son said, "Get frustrated. But don't get *too* frustrated." And you know what? I believe we're really going to need his advice to dodge hopelessness in the days ahead.

Thanks for keeping it real, son. Let's have a playdate today.

A Ten Hour Road Trip to Cross Political Divides

by Mónica Guzmán

Sherman County, Oregon, sits just south of the Washington border, east of the Cascades. Fewer than 2,000 people live in its 831 square miles. Stand on one of the hills near Moro, the county seat, and you'll see wheat fields all around—and maybe some tall wind turbines.

Sherman County has very little in common with Seattle and King County. And yet, we're connected: It's the nearest county to ours that voted exactly opposite us in the presidential election. While 74 percent of King County voters went for Clinton, 74 percent of Sherman County voters went for Trump.

So on Saturday, about twenty of us King County residents took a 10-hour road trip to pay the people of Sherman County a visit.

We called the trip "Melting Mountains: An Urban-Rural Gathering." Sandy Macnab, a just-retired Sherman and Wasco County agricultural agent who planned the event with us, came up with the name. It refers to the snowmelt that runs down the mountains dividing the eastern and western parts of our states, nourishing the land below.

We like the metaphor. And though we know we can't melt the political and cultural "mountains" that divide our two counties in an afternoon—red vs. blue, liberal vs. conservative, rural vs. urban—we figured we might help people take a first step.

We pulled up to Oregon State University's Sherman County Extension Office a little after 11 a.m. About four hours, one meal, and many conversations later, we said goodbye to the sixteen Sherman County residents we'd met to start the long drive back home.

The people who took part in the discussions told each other whom they'd voted for, revealed their stance on some big issues, talked about the hopes and concerns they had about their country over the next few years, and practiced listening to each other for minutes at a time (with instructions to not interrupt one another).

Here's how they thought it went.

"I wasn't sure what to expect." said Jennifer Zimmerlee, who is from Sherman County. "I can't lie—there was a little trepidation."

In one exercise, people from Sherman and King Counties paired off for a series of one-on-one conversations. In each of those, one person asked the other about his or her political hopes, concerns, and values and listened to the response. Then, they switched.

"I was afraid it'd be a lot more Clinton/Trump stuff," said Jennifer, who voted for third-party candidate Gary Johnson. "Instead what we got was some really nice guided discussions on the fact that even though how we approach problems is very different, in the end we truly are looking for the same thing."

The group came to that shared purpose early in the event, when everyone took turns introducing themselves. People in both counties agreed our divides had turned ugly, that they wanted to learn from each other, that this could be a start. "There's a lot I don't know about my own country," one person said.

There's a lot that has to happen before people unfamiliar with someone else's lifestyle can really understand it. Knowing that left Darren Padget, a fourth-generation Sherman County wheat farmer, a little disappointed.

"No one went out in the street and protested or had a baseball bat and did bad things," said Darren, who serves as chair of the Oregon Wheat Commision. "That was the positive of the day—having a civil conversation."

The negative, he said, is that he didn't get an opportunity to connect that deeply with city dwellers about how he lives his life. When he introduced himself, he pointed to the sandwiches people were eating for lunch. "If you knew what it took to get that simple sandwich on your plate . . ." he'd said then, to murmurs of thoughtful agreement from residents of both Sherman and King counties in the room.

"I would have appreciated a better opportunity to explain to them what we do and why we do it," he said.

Darren said his health care costs jumped 426 percent in the last few years and regulations like the "Waters of the United States" rule, which President Trump ordered the EPA to remove last month, are hurting his business.

"That's why I support Donald Trump and not Hillary Clinton," Darren said. "I didn't think either of them was a very good candidate, to be honest with you."

Jordan Goldwarg came from King County with his husband, Sam, and would have voted for Clinton if he could have. Jordan, who grew up in Canada, became a U.S. citizen just a few weeks ago.

At one point during the one-on-one discussions, Jordan heard the person he was paired with from Sherman County share a viewpoint on LGBTQ rights that made him uncomfortable.

The person made it clear, he said, that she had no problem with gay people. "But for me, as someone who is gay, the general tone of the conversations and the things she was saying that affect my life and the lives of a lot of people that I know—it was just difficult to hear that," Jordan said.

Jordan wished he'd had more time to unpack the divisions that turned up. But he didn't want to stop listening.

"I really value the opportunity to have conversations with people who seem very different from me, to be able to understand their experiences more and develop empathy with them," said Jordan, who is the regional director for a nonprofit that brings together people of different faiths.

"It seems this is exactly the kind of experience I'd been wanting to have, and didn't know how to find."

Like many people around Seattle, Leah Greenbaum woke up shocked November 9th. For weeks she consumed online and social media, trying to make sense of the election results through news articles and the explanations they laid out.

"Going to Sherman County and being in person, I think, I was surprised by the complexity of the stories I heard," she said. They made sense to her in a way that the online stories she'd read could not.

"To stand in front of someone and hear them speak with passion and feeling about what they believe, you sort of can't help but expand your own sense of empathy and humanity," Leah said.

Leah is a graduate student at the University of Washington's Evans School of Public Policy and Governance. When she heard people from Sherman County talk about how certain regulations and policies affected them, she asked herself how she could make sure the policies she works on are always informed by people's actual experiences.

"I want to get out there and talk to primary sources from now on," she said. "I love the media, my best friends are journalists . . . but I'm not going to look for easy answers anymore."

Others came away with things they wanted to do next:

- Jennifer said she planned to email every person who came from King County and shared their contact info to thank them for coming down.

- Darren said he's going to follow up with a couple he met from King County, and send them photos and material to continue a conversation they started on the Waters of the U.S. rule. "We [farmers] need to tell our story as much as we can," he said.

- Jordan said he wants to think about more ways to bridge urban and rural communities in his interfaith work.

And for us at *The Evergrey*? We're going to look for ways to help keep these conversations going. Tomorrow, we'll be sharing a few more perspectives, in their own words, from people who took part in "Melting Mountains."

And we want to find more ways to facilitate conversations among people who disagree.

"I know that when people pay attention to how they're speaking and listening to one another and really make an attempt to understand, remarkable things can happen," said Bob Stains, a conversation facilitator who advised us on this event.

On that, we agree.

An Authentic Invitation

by Marilee Jolin

I stopped talking to my parents about politics in 2001. By that point, the chasm between us had just gotten too wide. It didn't seem worth the effort—or the risk. I feared impassioned arguments. I feared derision and judgment. I feared damaging the relationship.

And, unfortunately, took a certain amount of ego-boosting pride in not attempting. "I can't talk to my parents *at all*," I'd say to my progressive, liberal friends, rolling my eyes. I'd exaggerate the extent of the conservative, evangelical fanaticism I experienced in church growing up. I'd wear my martyr badge with pride at how far *I'd* come, inferring how impossible it is for the less-enlightened to make that arduous journey.

I'm embarrassed now, remembering those conversations; embarrassed at how self-righteous and self-congratulatory I was. And how unfair it was to my parents because, in truth, I hadn't even given them a chance. I condemned them without ever having invited them.

In the lead-up to the 2016 election, I still couldn't bring myself to talk to my parents—even as it became more and more likely Donald Trump would be elected. I told myself that since our state's electoral votes would never go to him, it didn't matter—even if they voted Trump.

But it did matter. Not because of the electoral college—because I was distancing myself from my family, missing my foremost opportunity to live out my beliefs and ignoring my responsibility to educate the people in my life. Because I was excluding and isolating, instead of inviting.

Leave it to European Dissent[1] to not let me get away with that.

. . .

It was a few weeks after Trump's election and the church fellowship hall was packed. I tried counting all the people crammed together—even after opening the heavy wooden doors to the sanctuary so we could spread out a bit—and lost track around 500. There were many more than that.

The energy in the room was palpable. For many people, it was their first meeting and the combination of nerves, guilt, anticipation and anger was thick in the air. These white folks were feeling some real feelings and seriously unsure what to do with it all.

As always, the small group discussions were the most impacting.

Sitting uncomfortably in my folding chair listening to the other white folks in my discussion group share about the difficulties and joys of talking to family members with different political beliefs, I realized, with chagrin and shame, that I'd never even considered talking to my parents about race in America.

In listening to the other white folks at that meeting, I knew I couldn't stay silent anymore. If I can't talk to my family, who can I talk to? How can I pretend I'm working for social justice, resisting this racist regime, if I'm not willing to do the work in my own family?

So with their encouragement ringing in my ears and a belly-full of conviction, I went online to order some books.

---

1   European Dissent is a collective of white folks which exists to, "actively analyze and change the ways we as whites participate in racism personally, culturally, and institutionally. We make a commitment to undo racism personally, in our families, social life, workplaces and community work." From *European Dissent National Statement*

Ever the non-confrontational Seattleite, I failed to start an actual conversation that Thanksgiving holiday. Instead, I waited till Friday morning when everyone was packing up. Then I removed the three books I'd brought: Michelle Alexander's *The New Jim Crow*, Ta-Nehisi Coates' *Between the World and Me*, and bell hooks' *Ain't I a Woman?* I carefully pulled them from my bag, placed them gently on the kitchen counter and walked away.

It was not a *Chariots of Fire* moment by any stretch. I did not push past the clutching panic to force out words I knew needed speaking. I didn't have an earth-shattering conversation with tears and yelling that changed my view of myself forever. Honestly, I took the easiest way out humanly possible.

But the beauty is that it worked. And, I believe, it worked because I didn't push myself too far. I didn't take a flying leap off a 12-foot cliff into raging rapids—just slowly ascended the stairs into the 4-foot chlorinated pool. I didn't try to turn 180 degrees in my passive-aggressive, conflict-phobic family structure, just a small pivot toward authenticity.

It was a gentle pivot. But an honest one. It was a genuine invitation.

My dad picked up the books and said, "Are these for me?" I said, "Yup! For you and Mom." And then, quickly—before I could chicken out: "These books have been profoundly meaningful to me so I wanted to share them with you and I hope we can talk about them."

• • •

How often do our national political struggles cause us to think so far outside ourselves, so far away from home, that we become overly focused on the extremes and forget about the painful systemic racism embedded within our families and ourselves? We get caught up in the idea of forcefully changing minds or "defeating the opposition" and neglect the simple but difficult conversations in our own families. Conversations that, for many of us, would be with the "white moderates" Dr. King wrote of from the Birmingham Jail who are "more devoted to order than justice".

In the wake of Trump's election, I was challenged to take my first, mincing, embarrassing steps toward those important conversations. I fumbled and hemmed and hawed and took the easy way out, but I did it.

And what has come of this attempt is pure beauty. Because, beyond my wildest imaginings, my parents' worlds were also rocked by Michelle Alexander, Ta-Nehisi Coates and bell hooks. My father has left me far in the dust as he devours book after book: Michael Eric Dyson, Cornell West, James Baldwin. What began as me loaning him my favorite authors has now become a growing pile of books next to my nightstand as I strive to keep pace. He's starting a book group at his church with *The New Jim Crow* and has shared this important book with friends and family, inviting folks into the conversation I never would've asked.

And possibly, I think, that's how a truly cross-political movement builds. Because my father still watches Fox News. I haven't changed his mind about every topic and I likely won't. Because ultimately it isn't about changing minds—it's about building relationships and inviting people in. And so the movement grows. One fumbling book exchange at a time.

Finding a Collective Movement in "Progressive" Seattle

Three National Experts Feed Seattle's Social Justice Scene

by Renea Harris-Peterson & emily warren

Seattle, celebrated for its progressive stance on many issues, still struggles to push past the facade of "liberalism" into true work towards equity. Lack of rent control, the police force being under investigation, woefully underfunded education, and the proposal to build a new youth incarceration facility are just a few examples of how the city has fallen short on its promises of progressivism.

Recently, Seattle hosted two Black academics, Angela Davis and Bryan Stevenson, and a White academic, Peggy McIntosh, to inspire audiences around issues of social justice and to quell discontent in the aftermath of Trump's election. To some extent those two goals were achieved; however, it is useful to consider the ways these goals in fact reinforce Seattle's so-called progressivism, inhibiting real and meaningful change. The experiences we had at these three lectures were starkly different and spoke to the characteristics of their audiences. We'd like to shed light on some of these dynamics in hopes of disrupting the status quo of activism in this city and moving towards a more collective movement.

We (Renea and emily) decided to write this essay because our feelings after each event were so varied and we wanted to make sense of it. Even though Davis, Stevenson, and McIntosh were all addressing relatively similar issues, they addressed those issues quite differently. We wanted to dig deeper to find out what was really going on, both for ourselves and for our community—as clichéd as it may sound the intent of each talk may not have been congruent with the impact. Our conversations following these events were rich, and we felt as if our life experiences and how we came to understand and process these events was worth sharing:

I (Renea) am a 17 year old biracial woman, and I was born and raised here in Seattle. Being a teenager allows me to bring new perspectives and energy to the movement. I have lived in many neighborhoods in the area and have a good sense of the different communities and cultural nuances.

I (emily) am a math teacher of nearly 20 years, who is relatively new to Seattle and am seeing the city with fresh eyes. I am a White woman who has spent many years trying to understand the ways in which my Whiteness and being a woman impact my experience as well as how I engage in equity work.

About the same time Davis came to Seattle to speak, I (Renea) chose to write a paper at school about how sexism in the Black Panther Party contributed to their downfall. I finally got to learn about people who looked like me and were doing all the things I want to do. One figure I researched deeply was Angela Davis—someone I feel a particular connection with since one of the first times my aunt saw my hair picked out into a full fro, she said I looked like a young Angela Davis. I have carried that moment with me ever since, reminding myself that I can use the work and foundation of my elders to move the movement forward and create real change. As a part of this process, I learned how to not view myself as a woman and as Black as separate identities, and this was really transformative. As I was planning how I was going to reinvigorate The Black Panther Party, I found out that Angela Davis would be coming to Town Hall, and it seemed like fate.

Angela Davis was welcomed to Seattle as the keynote speaker for the MLK Unity Day, an annual event celebrating Martin Luther King Jr's continued legacy and vision. The free lecture and program was hosted by the City of Seattle, Mayor Ed Murray, Council President Bruce A. Harrell and members of the Seattle City Council, and other city departments.

While at the talk, I saw an old classmate, my brother's friend from high school, my old teacher, and my cousin scattered around the audience. It felt like a family reunion with cousins you barely know in attendance, though you still share a connection.

The band was playing the music that my mom listens to, the music that makes her close her eyes, shake her head, and feel it in her soul. The audience, an estimated eight hundred and fifty, was dressed casually, and the majority seemed like they were in the middle class.

The event's rich programming set the perfect stage for Davis. Lucille Hampton, an elder from the Dkhw'Duw'Absh (Duwamish) tribe in Washington, paid tribute to the stolen indigenous land that we're all currently occupying.

Matt Remle and his two sons from the Hunkpapa Lakota tribe performed, reminding us that we must stand up to injustice everywhere and stand with Standing Rock. Then the Seattle Youth Poet Laureate, Leija Farr, a young Black woman, recited her poem titled "Black Woman Chronicles" and Seattle city council-member Bruce Harrell introduced Davis.

When Davis spoke, we both felt like everyone in the room was keyed into every moment, every syllable; it was precious and impossible to reproduce. At the other events, people were on their phones, tweeting or posting on Facebook, but, listening to Davis, hardly anyone was—not because it wouldn't have been accepted (it definitely would have been), but because no one wanted to take their eyes off her.

Often, she spoke directly to the youth and activists in the community, and as she spoke, snaps, clapping and "mmhmms" floated through the air. She was always straight-to-the-point, which is expected of her. I think this made some people, like Harrell, nervous because she wasn't going to sugarcoat her opinions, especially around the new youth jail. She said the words "NO NEW YOUTH JAIL," something Stevenson couldn't commit to and McIntosh didn't even address. (When Stevenson made reference to Seattle's controversial building of a new youth jail, he kept it appropriately mild for the audience. He said, "I hear there's a narrative around building a new jail . . . I would love to see

Seattle to be a leader in this area. We need more counselors and health professionals.")

It was powerful to be surrounded by Black folks, all committed to the cause, and to see future versions of myself (Renea) at different stages of my life. For me (emily), I was one of the few White folks in attendance, but I was inspired by Davis' vision and connected to her focus on the collective. I simultaneously felt like an outsider and as a part of the movement. I held this tension gently and was appreciative to be in the space.

What struck us was that it didn't seem as if Davis' overall message was particular to her audience; she could have given that speech in front of many different kinds of audiences. Because Davis seemed to be liberated from her audience, it allowed her to present an authentic self, and helped her speak her truth in ways that the others could not.

From the personal narratives, to the #NoNewYouthJail movement, to capitalism, and to Palestine, she covered a large range of topics, and hit the personal, interpersonal, institutional, and systemic levels of oppression. Her message was how we might imagine real change, focusing on the importance of collective struggle: "Change happens because we are able to imagine ourselves as much more than we are as individuals." She lifts up different voices in her collective by tying these bigger issues back to local and personal life experiences.

Davis also explained how we should draw encouragement and inspiration from the past struggles for social justice, saying, "As we observe MLK Unity Day, we celebrate our potential as agents in a collective quest for freedom."

Her message was that MLK Unity Day is not only about celebrating the legacy of Martin Luther King Jr as an individual. It is also about recognizing that through him, we pay tribute to all the people who never surrendered to racism and inequality. By doing this, we acknowledge the people who have been rendered invisible by being poor, Black, or women. Similar to her message about Dr. King, she said, "People frequently mistakenly attribute force and power to me that I do not deserve because I simply stand here as evidence of the power of masses of people when they come together."

Her message about the collective is what the other two speakers missed. It takes more than thinking and tiny actions to create real change, and Davis addressed this by saying, "The only way forward is unending struggle."

While Bryan Stevenson also discussed how one can make a difference, his speech had a different message and feel. Stevenson was sponsored by Seattle Arts and Lectures (SAL) and co-presented by the *Seattle Times*, Seattle Pacific University, Seattle University, and The University of Washington. Stevenson's lecture was a part of a Literary\ Arts Series presenting "original talks by six outstanding authors whose works range from multi-award-winning novels and short stories to social commentaries and biographies." At Stevenson's talk, nearly everyone in the audience was dressed to a T!

There were a few people of color, with most of the attendees being white, and skewing to the older side. The 2500-seat hall was packed. The feel was formal, and the social "norming" around etiquette and audience behavior was palpable.

After sitting down, the two White women sitting next to us spoke loudly about their hopes that people would quit with their texting. As I (emily) had my phone out, I wondered if they were talking about me.

Once the program began, the host encouraged the audience to post to Facebook and Twitter using a hashtag; we got dirty looks throughout from the women sitting next to us. Posting live via Facebook or Twitter during an experience is a way to share and democratize knowledge, particularly when the entrance fee is $20 a ticket.

While the video of Davis' talk was posted online in several places, we weren't sure if Stevenson's would be. It turns out that it wasn't, and after we requested a video or transcript of Stevenson's talk from SAL, we were told that it was because of "the contract with Stevenson/The Speakers Bureau that we do not have or pass on the transcript." (Similarly, when we reached out the The Graduate School at UW, they let us know that "unfortunately, we do not have video/audio records available, or a transcript of the evening.")

The contradictory nature of Stevenson's host encouraging the audience to post on social media to share the experience and the other aspects of our experience, such as the dirty looks from our row-mates, high priced ticket, audience make-up, such an extravagant location, and not making video or transcripts available, sent mixed messages about who really should have access to this event.

Other social norming was on display throughout Stevenson's talk, from applauding only at "appropriate" times and the pressure to give a "proper" standing ovation, which was in stark contrast to the feel of Davis's talk. This "etiquette" reminded us of what must have been at play nearly three years ago when two Black activists, Marissa Johnson and Mara Jacqueline Willaford, interrupted Bernie Sanders at a Seattle rally and were booed relentlessly and criticized in the media in the weeks following. White folks want their liberalism, but only on their own terms.

The entire front section at Stevenson's event, and many of the more prominent seats in the balcony, were reserved for "special guests." While we are not able to say for sure who had access to these seats, what we can say was that they were very well-dressed, older, and mostly White. It certainly did not look like the seats were reserved for marginalized community members. The front two rows in McIntosh's speech were reserved for students in two academic classes. Neither compared to the inspirational energy emanating from the youth organizers from Block the Bunker, EPIC, and Seattle Block Book Club, who were sitting front and center at Davis' lecture.

Interestingly, Seattle's Youth Poet Laureate, Leija Farr, also spoke at Stevenson's talk; she recited a poem titled "For Black Boys." A White woman introduced Stevenson, highlighting his many prestigious degrees and credentials and framing his work with one of his points of action: hope.

This served to pull the audience in, to keep them comfortable. As we were soon to find out, Stevenson's message was also crafted in a way to make it palatable to a White audience. Stevenson skillfully wove personal stories with statistics and a larger analysis of the current system of mass incarceration.

His speech outlined a vision to take action against the injustices of our current system of incarceration: (a) change one's proximity to suffering, (b) resist and change narratives based on fear and anger, (c) make the decision to do uncomfortable things and (d) don't lose hope. The message was clearly crafted for the audience in front of him. For example, marginalized people live in a constant state of discomfort, so the call to "do uncomfortable things" was a call to a largely White and wealthy audience.

While this is a noble message, there's also a danger in taking it only at face value. His point of staying in proximity to suffering is dangerous because it has a close relationship to gentrification. He did not go into enough detail about how to successfully be in close proximity to suffering, leaving the audience to figure it out themselves. White people in Seattle do not have a problem with colonizing spaces for people of color, and it is important to examine the relationship between this close proximity and gentrification. In addition, the danger in focusing only on hope works to center White comfort in equity work and disconnect White people from the real pain, terror, and horror of White supremacy. Maintaining a balance between hope and honest examination of the dark side of White supremacy is important, but that balance was off in Stevenson's talk. Only at the end of his talk did Stevenson discuss reconciling with the past, for instance, how Germany and Rwanda were models for looking honestly at the national past and how the US has fallen short in our reckoning with our genocidal past, both with Native Americans and with slavery. Stevenson then talked about his forthcoming project: a Lynching museum. All that being said, the scales were weighted towards hope.

Like Davis, Stevenson worked to lift up voices that have traditionally been silenced, specifically, by relaying personal stories of representing clients in the criminal justice system. One of the most powerful was about a Black man named Avery Jenkins, who suffered from mental illness and had a history of being passed through the foster system since age two. Although Jenkins had committed a serious crime, Stevenson argued that his difficult past and intellectual disabilities (Stevenson's words) had not been taken into account. Jenkins had not received the support and services he needed throughout his life. Stevenson's analysis of how the system not only targets Black and Brown folks, but how those with mental illness are particularly vulnerable, was a way that Stevenson was able to amplify traditionally silenced voices.

That being said, this story was intertwined with a story about a White racist correctional officer, who, by the end of the story, had shifted in his perspective towards Stevenson. This juxtaposition first made the predominately White audience just uncomfortable enough with the realities of a Black, disabled man in this country, then followed with a hook of hope for their own salvation. The correctional officer, while real, was the extreme stereotype of a "racist," complete with pick-up truck and confederate flags. For a White, liberal, upper-class audience member, this is an easy way to distance oneself from Whiteness; that is clearly NOT ME. And, yet, there is still a lingering wondering . . . is there a part of that officer that is me?

Luckily, Stevenson ends the story with the officer shaking his hand, thanking him for his work. The officer, as it turns out, has had his own run-in with the foster care system and has a change of heart towards Jenkins and Stevenson. This display of redemption allows for a collective sigh from the White audience: there can be redemption after blatant displays of racism.

So, while Stevenson was able to lead White folks to the discomforts of Black and Brown realities, there was the safety net of seeing White folks humanized, as well. The way Stevenson lifted up "voices rendered invisible" was different than Davis, who tended to be more abstract. Stevenson's story-telling about individual people brought people into the struggle. His strong academic background and credentials only helped to make him a legitimate voice, one who is able to be heard by While folks and subsequently celebrated.

Another voice able to be heard by White folks was the third speaker: Peggy McIntosh. McIntosh was hosted by the University of Washington's Graduate School and UW Alumni Association, and she was a part of a series called Equity & Difference: Privilege, hosted by The Graduate School at the University of Washington and funded by the Walker-Ames Fund, the Jessie and John Danz Fund, and the Mary Ann and John D. Mangels Fund.

Seeing Peggy McIntosh provided a final important piece in how we thought about speakers on activism. The whole experience made us feel like we were actually at university! The audience was fairly racially diverse, though it was still primarily White. There was also more age diversity, and most in the crowd were casually dressed. A White man introduced McIntosh, citing her many accomplishments and prestigious degrees. McIntosh opened by discussing her road to equity work. She talked about her move from wanting to be popular (fear-based) to wanting to be useful (riskier, but more gratifying): "The one thing I hope you take away from this is that this kind of work is transformative."

This message was useful in reminding us to keep equity work rooted in oneself; too often White folks do equity for people of color, which perpetuates power imbalances and White Saviorism. The danger, however, is that this kind of self-work can quickly turn to naval-gazing, when not challenged.

McIntosh then helped the audience move from a binary understanding of people in power to a more nuanced one: instead of being caught in a trap of seeing a person (or oneself) as nice OR oppressive, one can see that person as nice AND oppressive. This allows one to see the wholeness of a person while also allowing us to pull ourselves into the problem. McIntosh then discussed her seminal piece "White Privilege: Unpacking the Invisible Knapsack," a list of 26 examples of how White privilege operates in McIntosh's life on a daily basis.

She then talked about ways she tries to use her White Privilege, citing examples from another piece of hers, "White Privilege: An Account to Spend." Many of her points were focused on the individual, such as reexamining hiring practices and using your own voice in hiring committees or choosing to live on less money so you can give money to social justice organizations. Only one that she spoke of, visiting the police station to protest, involved a true collective, but even then McIntosh talked about using one's own voice, she advised "Say more than you think you have in you."

While McIntosh's storytelling brought people in (as did Stevenson's), her stories were mostly about her own individual experience, while Stevenson's stories were about his work and the stories of those folks not typically told. Davis' stories also spoke to her own experience, which, in this case, is important because stories such as hers are not always lifted up, heard, or celebrated.

Even though McIntosh's speech was primarily encouraging individual reflection, we also know that her professional work balances individual and community work. In "White Privilege: An Account to Spend," McIntosh writes: "I organize projects, invest time and money, read, write letters and emails, intervene, spread the word, campaign, work with others against injustice and try to influence policy. It is a mixture of raising my own awareness and trying to change the social fabric as well." In truth, McIntosh has moved to the institutional through her work in *Seeking Educational Equity and Diversity* (SEED).

The program trains teachers to lead sessions in their own schools; much of this work is in the collective. What was missing from this particular talk, however, was McIntosh encouraging White folks to join the struggle not only on a personal and interpersonal level, but on an institutional and collective level as well. Academics can get stuck in their heads, and while her talk provided good context and framing, it failed to connect to the collective struggle. Academia is largely White and elite, so it often leaves out the lived experiences of people of color. It's important for academics and intellectuals to push out of the internal and into action.

Seeing Peggy McIntosh was important for me (emily) to connect with an elder who reflected who I could be, but it was also a reminder for me not to get stuck in my head. For me (Renea), I felt a disconnect related to race. While the talk was interesting and I learned a lot, I still felt a compartmentalization between my White identity, being a woman, and me being Black; they weren't operating together. Seeing Davis, I could show up with all three. While both of us connected to Stevenson's message, it was hard for us to connect to him personally as a change-maker.

Ultimately, Davis' message was the importance of unending struggle in the collective, Stevenson's was that you can make a difference so don't lose hope, and McIntosh was to make personal transformation for the larger good. From our vantage point, Davis seemed to attract the activist, Stevenson, the financial elite, and McIntosh, the academic. While all three have a place in social justice, the latter two categories are most often White and have a great deal of privilege (our experiences at these events bore this out), and the danger is that talks like these serve to reinforce the disconnected and fragmented spheres that these groups operate in, which undermines a collective movement toward change.

So, what can be done? It starts with shifting the audiences at these kinds of events. How can organizers be intentional about getting a diverse audience to their events? Could SAL organizers have put aside the front section for more people of color and activists, like organizers for Angela Davis did? How can we get more White folks to see Davis without it being at the expense of the youth or risk gentrifying the space? This could be a part of seeing other perspectives and not just catering to a certain audience; if the audiences were more diverse maybe we would shift more to the collective.

Changing audiences is a step, but it is not real change. How can we re-envision change to the collective? How can we move from the individual, which both Stevenson and McIntosh emphasized, to a more collective vision? How can White folks responsibly do the work, balancing self-examination with movement in the streets towards the collective? How do people of color exercise patience to meet people where they are in their understanding, allowing them to address others' humanity and engage with them? How can people of color maintain a balance of connection while not doing the work of White people? Where is the growth of White folks around the collective? Where is the growth for people of color around the collective? How can we see Stevenson and Davis not as a fracturing of the Black community, but part of the wholeness of the collective, while still providing important critiques?

One way we can see change in this area is to make our collective as intersectional as possible, including the many different identities that a person brings. It is important to reflect on the learning of folks of color, as well as White folks, because it is doesn't hold them accountable to the personal and societal change that they can create. This underscores the importance of hearing multiple perspectives, both in hearing speakers and engaging in political action, but also in one's organization, friend group, and community.

We are in a ripe moment, historically. Now that White people are getting used to being in the streets for the women's march and the science march, it's time to call them into the streets for issues they SAY they care about such as racial inequality and mass incarceration. In fact, as we sit in this cafe writing this article, a White woman at the table next to us is talking about how moving it was to read Stevenson's *Just Mercy*.

We need to help White folks see the link between these issues in the abstract and how they manifest practically: #NoNewYouthJail, #Blacklivesmatter, unfair policing practices, rent control, and affordable housing. This may mean a financial sacrifice for those who own and control property in this city. Beyond people taking the streets, we need to reflect on our spheres of power and how we can influence change in a real way, from supporting and voting for candidates that support these issues, using what political capital we have to influence those who make the decisions, and working to transform our organizations to make real change. This is all part of the collective struggle.

We see this essay as a part of this collective struggle as we, Renea and emily, continue to engage around issues of social justice and equity. We have marched together, we have worked in the math classroom together, we have attended events together, we struggled through this article and its analysis together, we have stumbled on our own areas of growth together, we laugh together, and we continue to learn with one another. This is all part of the struggle.

"Let us remember that so much of what is important, so much of what has acquired significance, historical significance, has been achieved through mass struggle . . . We have come to realize that the only way forward is unending struggle." ~ Angela Davis

International Workers of Natural Foods Grocery Stores, Unite!

by Alex Gallo-Brown

When I think back, it was probably riding the bus home with my co-worker that did it. We barely knew each other's names, but we worked in the same department; she was upset, and I let her know that I would listen. Her kid was sick, she already had nine points, her meth-head brother was at home, and if she missed even one more day, they would probably let her go . . .

I had been at the job less than a month but I knew that something was wrong. I got the job as a cook in a natural foods grocery store outside Seattle with the intention of subsidizing my creative writing. But politics, especially in the wake of the election of 2016, were very much on my mind. Fortunately, my new employer appeared to be a force for good. It believed in "people, planet, and profits," presumably in equal measure. It prized cultural and racial diversity and strived to reduce waste. It was good to its workers, providing benefits (healthcare, paid time off, and sick leave), "lifestyle scheduling," and profit-share. It gave back to the community.

It didn't take long, however, for a different picture to emerge. On my third week, I was scheduled to work seven days in a row. "Lifestyle scheduling," then, appeared to be more of a suggestion than a hard-and-fast rule. The managers' style was brusque, top-down, and impersonal. And the benefits were not available for the first three months, which meant that if we called in sick, we accrued "attendance points" at the rate of three each absence, two every time we missed an hour or more, and one when time we arrived six minutes late. After we accumulated ten points, for any reason, even a legitimate illness, over the course of six months, we would be fired.

If that policy seemed harsh, the reality was even harsher: We could be fired for any reason (even none) at any time. Since Washington is an "at will" employment state, employees without union protection serve at the whim of their employer; they can be hire and fired "at will." And at the natural foods grocery store, despite the progressive pose, we had no union. We were completely under management's control.

I was vaguely aware that it was a non-union store before I began, but it came fully to my attention after union organizers began visiting workers' homes. News of the activity trickled back to management, who responded by posting flyers in the break room, in the hallway, near the clock where we punched in. They were so sorry the union was harassing us. Under no circumstances were we to give out information about our co-workers. They were here to support us during this difficult time.

Those flyers made my blood boil. They hadn't asked *us* whether we wanted to be part of a union or not. They hadn't given us that choice. I had worked in a union grocery store before, and I knew the benefits that unionization could bring—better wages and benefits, a more reasonable attendance policy, representation in the workplace if management gave us a hard time. But there was broader political import, too. In a time of the populist authoritarianism of Trump, unions, in my mind, represented social democracy—they required people to imagine themselves as part of a larger social project in solidarity with people who they didn't personally know.

It was only a few days later that I spoke with my co-worker on the bus. If I had been on the fence before—I hadn't, but I had been busy: those rotisserie chickens weren't going to cook themselves—her story made my mind. I was in a more or less comfortable situation—a master's degree, some money in the bank, a supportive partner, middle-class friends. If they let me go, I could always find another job. My co-worker's situation was different. If she were fired because of attendance, it might have catastrophic consequences for her and her son.

I began reaching out to co-workers who I felt that I could trust. I started with a woman who I had bonded with in the break room over our shared antipathy to Trump.

What do you think about this union stuff? I asked her when no one was around. *Let's talk about that later,* she whispered, putting her finger to her lips. We exchanged phone numbers and quickly shuffled back to our posts.

That night, we discovered that our thinking was aligned. The store wasn't what we thought it was going to be. Despite the flowery rhetoric, the working conditions were unjust. It wasn't right that people were encouraged to come into work sick. Not right that workers could be terminated for any reason at any time. (Already we had seen a number of people come and go.) Not right that we were being subtly discouraged from joining the union. We decided to reach out to the organizers and see what they had to say.

Our first meeting was at a Mexican restaurant not far from the store. The organizers' method was inquisitive. They wanted to know about how our experience had been. We told them about the attendance policy and asked if that was something that a union could improve. It was certainly within the realm of bargaining, they said. But to win a contract would be a real test. The store, which was part of a larger chain, was notoriously anti-union. Other workers had been fired for doing just this very thing. If we wanted to move forward, we should know that we were putting ourselves at risk.

My friend and I were undeterred. We weren't going to work at the grocery store forever, but while we were there we wanted to do what we could to help things improve.

With the organizers, we made calculations. There were somewhere between a hundred and a hundred and fifty employees at the store. To win a union, we would need at least thirty percent of that number (thirty to forty five people) to sign "union authorization cards" expressing support for an election. In the election we would need more than fifty percent (fifty one to seventy six people) to vote yes. So far, we had two.

We obviously had a daunting road ahead. I tried to think about how many people I knew well. As a cook, I was largely confined to the kitchen. I couldn't very well cavort over to produce and start chatting people up. My friend had more access to other departments. But still—seventy six people. It was almost difficult to imagine.

Still, what else could we do? Slink back to our corners? Look the other way? During the next week I raised the question awkwardly with my co-workers. The walk-in refrigerator became my office. I bantered with people among raw chicken and blocks of cheddar cheese. I started smoking again. When better then to talk to people about the union than when sharing fire in the cold?

The responses I got were mixed. One common concern was dues—people wanted to make sure they were getting a fair deal. Another was viability. Could we really get enough support? But the most common reaction was fear. They didn't want to upset management. They didn't want to go against the grain. One woman told me that if I didn't like the rules, I should find another job.

Over time, gradually, we built up support. At first two, then three, then five people committed to the cause. We met up at my house for dinner, or went out to restaurants for drinks. I found the meetings exciting. At the grocery store we often talked about building teamwork and community, but this was the real thing—genuine communion and solidarity across racial, class, and gender lines.

I'm not sure if management knew what we were up to. I suspect they probably did. They couldn't legally prevent us from organizing, but they could make their opinions clear. The CEO came and held an all-store meeting to address worker concerns. "We're not anti-union," she said, "we're non-union. We're comfortable with how we are." Our department manager told a co-worker, "The day this store goes union is the day that I will quit."

During a meeting with the store manager about a promotion, another co-worker was asked to describe his feelings about the union. While interrogation or intimidation is technically a violation of labor law, in order for an employer to face the consequences, the employee has to file a complaint. And my friend, who wanted to advance within the company, wasn't about to do that.

Over the course of my six months working there, I talked to dozens of workers about the union, many of whom expressed support. Getting them to meetings, on the other hand, was another story. They would tell me that they were going to be there and then not answer their phone. In a way, I couldn't blame them. Spend your day off, normally reserved for partners or kids or parents or friends, coordinating with co-workers to talk about work? It wasn't that bad. They could always find something else.

Something else that was almost certainly non-union. At a time when union membership is at its lowest level since the Great Depression (about 7 percent in the private sector and 40 percent in the public), job security for most American workers has become a thing of the past. And while unions are often talked about in their relation to inequality, equally important, in my mind, is the political consciousness that they can instill.

The ethic of a union is participation, empowerment, self-determination, and collaborative pride. It is about many different individuals coming together to speak in a collective voice. Is it any wonder that in this era of declining unions our politics have seen such a rightward shift? When people are expected to blindly defer to their authority at work, would it not make sense for them to be attracted to authoritarian government, too?

As for me, I was eventually let go. I called in sick a few times; I reached the maximum number of points allowed.

Whether I was fired for organizing, I suppose I'll never know.

My Time at Standing Rock

by Rashad Barber

I did not journey across the country to learn anything. I ventured to stand in solidarity with our Native relatives, but while I was at Standing Rock in the Oceti Sakowin Camp, I learned much, including the vastness of the camp.

I do not know what I thought I would see, but I was not expecting an entire valley filled with tents, teepees, campers, vehicles and people. I have been part of many demonstrations in opposition to unjust exploitation of peoples and planet, but I have never before been part of anything like Standing Rock.

There were thousands of people from all over the world, many of whom were represented on Flag Road, which seemed to go on forever identifying all the nations and peoples in solidarity with Oceti Sakowin (Seven Council Fires). This is the "proper name for the people commonly known as Sioux."

What I witnessed is that a shift is underway the likes of which we have not experienced since the time of the Black Panther Party for Self-Defense (BPP) and the American Indian Movement (AIM), when the world's oppressed peoples are uniting in a common cause: to end the harmful exploitation of our peoples and planet, and caring for our world and peoples in such a way that ten generations from now our descendants will inherit a healthy and vibrant world to share. And while such a shift in culture is neither without opposition or complications, it is nonetheless beautiful to see coming to fruition.

This level of unity among the oppressed peoples must be terrifying to the repressive state regime because it is losing its legitimacy and control, and people are losing faith in this state's ability to manage our world. This is evinced by the harmful and repressive actions the state has engaged in to retain its control of the people and the situation. The state has enacted counterinsurgency tactics and technology against its own people in the worst of ways.

From the targeted arresting of people, to the excessive use of lethal force, to the eviction of peoples from their lands, to the complete disregard of humanity of indigenous peoples and people of color; the entire operation is laden with human rights violations.

The right to peaceably assemble and to the freedom of religion are not only guaranteed by the U.S. Constitution (First Amendment), but also the Universal Declaration of Human Rights (Article 18; Article 19; Article 20). Furthermore, Article 9, of the UNDHR states that "no one shall be subject to arbitrary arrest, detention, or exile." Article 5, of the UNDHR, says that no one shall be subjected to cruel and unusual punishment; which should entail being sprayed with water from fire hoses when it is twenty degrees outside, or shot in the head with rubber bullets for praying on your own lands.

Not that it needs to be mentioned, but in case people have forgotten, cruel and unusual punishment is also protected against by the Eighth Amendment to the United States Constitution. Using intimidation and legalized terrorism is not managing, it is tyranny and it is out of control. The problem lies in the reality that this sort of behavior has been normalized in the United States when the state is interacting with indigenous peoples, people of color, and active political dissent from the harmful practices of this state and its agents. However, the oppressed peoples are uniting as the legitimacy of the state is faltering and we are being joined by those who are also losing faith in the state's motivations and the results of its decisions.

Oceti Sakowin Camp is a prayer ceremony on treaty land (Treaty of Fort Laramie 1868); that is, the land the camp is on and where Energy Transfer Partners LP is constructing the Dakota Access Pipeline (DAPL) belongs to Oceti Sakowin. First, if someone were to come to a home belonging to either you or me and started destroying things, especially that which our ancestors or predecessors left to us, we would most likely stand in physical opposition to the intrusion and destruction. And we would be well within our rights to do so. It is a twisted way of thinking about development and progress—the doctrine of Manifest Destiny—that informs people's perception that the manner in which our Native relatives have chosen to be stewards of the land is neither efficient nor correct.

Notwithstanding that false perception, this land belongs to Oceti Sakowin and the infringement into their land is no different than an intrusion into our homes. Thus, when physical opposition has occurred, the people who engaged in these acts have been completely and entirely justified in doing such. In fact, the actual motivation and justification for the Second Amendment to the United States Constitution was to protect against the arbitrary and tyrannical abuses of power by the state over the people. The fact that it mentions weapons only provides one of the means by which this may, or should be, accomplished. The spirit of the amendment is that state repression of free and equal peoples is not to be tolerated when the repression is unjust.

Yet, while that is not only the law and the right of the people, the state, the corporations, and the media has sought to villainize and delegitimize the actions of Water Protectors, as if they believe something else, or would have behaved differently should this have happened to their homes and their families.

Painting the entire camp and opposition movement with broad strokes as riotous villains, in an attempt to discredit Oceti Sakowin and gain legitimacy for state tyranny is unacceptable. These actions are wrong and unaccountable to the Amerikan people and the people of the world. And yet, however justified physical opposition is, the majority of the opposition, and the vast majority of the people at Standing Rock are in prayer, and have been for most of the time the camp has existed.

Every morning before sunrise, a water ceremony occurs that is usually led by elders who are women. The people at Oceti Sakowin Camp are called to the Sacred Fire to participate in the ceremony as the people first ask to commune with the Creator, before asking the Creator to protect the headwaters of the Midwest. Many people from Amerika are not familiar with prayer in the form of song and dance because many of us come from a Judeo-Christian background, and so, it may not be immediately recognized that a prayer ceremony is occurring, but that does not alter the immense power that is felt participating after being invited into one of the ceremonies.

From the Sacred Fire after the initial prayers are completed, the people are led to the water (Cannon Ball River) to bless and pray for the water that heals our bodies and our souls. As the sun rises we are standing on the shores of the waters giving thanks for the resource and element that provides so much for us and all that lives on the planet we share. Starting the day in a thankful spirit of gratitude for a precious and limited resource has the impact of directing our whole day, and shifted my thoughts from what I need to take for myself, and instead focused them on what I have to offer.

The time I spent at Oceti Sakowin Camp led me to re-conceptualize my perception of direct action, even as a seasoned activist. Often direct action is referred to as a demonstration. For example, when a Black Lives Matter protest occurs on Black Friday, in any city—challenging the very institutions of a capitalistic economy that buttresses and profits from the prison industrial complex and by extension the brutality of police, and the school to prison pipeline—the objective is to interrupt. Wherein there may be lockdowns, blocked traffic, or interruptions of broadcasts.

However, at Oceti Sakowin, when the people leave camp to any location, it is in prayer just like the morning Water Ceremony. The prayers are not discriminatory, but universal, which means that the people are praying for the health of the water not only for Oceti Sakowin, but also for those parts of the repressive state regime spraying Water Protectors with fire hoses in twenty degree weather. Behaviors with these motivations in other settings have often been referred to as acts of unconditional love and bring to mind the Civil Rights Movement of the Black Liberation Era. I know many of the stories, but have not exactly been able to bring myself to love those I have seen and felt as my enemies as they continued to harm me and my peoples.

Growing up, I was racially profiled by police more times than I can count or even remember, but a few situations stand out. I was pulled over for nothing besides driving while Black and when the cop could find nothing else to charge me with, not a tail light, not a failed signal, not an invalid license, he placed some sort of light detector on my tinted windows to try to find anything to justify his harassment of me.

Another account was when my father called the police because some of our neighbors were threatening to kill my brother and me when we were eight and nine, respectively. When the police came they arrested my father. I can remember walking home from high school with my book bag, only to have a cop car jump the curb and come to a screeching halt in front of me. The officer slammed me against a wall and searching through my school books, only to find school books.

And one night when I was walking down the sidewalk, two plain clothes cops simply decided not to identify themselves. Instead they beat me almost to death before hauling me off to jail for absolutely nothing. I did not receive an apology, nor was I given bus fare home after being released from their custody to walk miles home at three-thirty in the morning in the middle of winter.

I recount these personal experiences now only to evince that my hatred for the institution of police is not only systemic, but also personal. When we arrived at the camp we were asked to set these feelings aside and to pray for the police, the army, the militias, and the mercenaries suppressing the people at Standing Rock. This was difficult for me, as it was for many others, too. Then I heard a report about one of the leaders of the International Indigenous Youth Council, speaking directly to how the people interact with the police during a prayer ceremony;

"It is our duty not to dehumanize others, as we seek to establish our own humanity."

What I learned from this is that I am no better if I create the same trauma that I am seeking to overcome. I cannot become my enemy and still expect to overcome the oppression I suffer from my enemy. The means must be consistent with the ends, if the ends are to be just.

So, while the people at Standing Rock are completely justified in mounting an armed resistance to the Dakota Access Pipeline, the Army Corps of Engineers, and the suppressive agents using counterinsurgency tactics against the people, they are in fact, praying for all of us. I have never experienced this amount of love and forgiveness. I have read about and studied it, I have heard stories from the Foot Soldiers of the Civil Rights Movement, but I have never felt it.

This is the spirit of the people that our government has permitted helicopters and planes to fly over the camp surveilling, and is suspected of spraying chemicals on, day and night. This is the spirit of the people that the government is utilizing cell phone suppression and corruption technology upon. This is the spirit of the people that the government is throwing concussion grenades at, shooting in the head with rubber bullets, unleashing the Long Range Sound Device, the LRAD sound cannon—the same technology used in Ferguson after the execution of Michael Brown—and spraying with water from fire hoses in twenty degree weather at; all of which are prefaced as non-lethal instruments, but when applied together and in the conditions they were used, are all individually lethal and are especially so in conjunction with one another. The state has been arresting, imprisoning, and nearly killing people for praying—on their own lands no less.

The state is a force to be reckoned with, many of us know this acutely well from first or second-hand experiences, and it must be confronted and challenged. There are also other complications that can and do often emerge when people who have been oppressed unite among themselves, and when the oppressed people unite with people who are from privileged classes. It is not the issues so much as how they are addressed that is truly important. At Oceti Sakowin Camp there was a lot of very positive and encouraging work being done to overcome much of this while simultaneously challenging neo-liberalism, capitalism, and state repression.

During orientation at Oceti Sakowin Camp on my first morning there we were told that we should not have come to learn, or to take anything because that is a continuation of the colonial apparatus. Yet, still, because so many people flooded into the camp over 'Thanksgiving' week, who were honestly concerned about what is and has been happening at Standing Rock, who were by no means prepared enough in a socially conscious manner for the work ahead, some instruction was necessary. I am a photographer and this has been a major component of the liberation work I have engaged in over the years. I am also a historian and a philosopher, and the three of these skills combined help me tell stories as objectively as possible.

During the orientation, the proctors mentioned that the act of taking a picture "take, take, take" is an act of colonization, which is all about the extraction of people, land, and resources. This was used as an analogy to us expecting to have time with Native elders who could "tell the history correctly" because people had "come to learn the truth" from the people most impacted.

Not realizing that the imposition of time, from primarily white folx, was another act of colonization playing itself out, many had rushed to the elders. Many people had also been walking through camp with their cameras out, snapping shots of people in front of their teepees, which is no different than standing on someone's lawn and pointing a camera into their home; taking, extracting, and feeling 'entitled' to do so.

This colonialist imperative of take all you can for yourself, this capitalist motif is precisely what the people at Oceti Sakowin Camp are opposed to. It is this colonialist imperative and capitalist motif that Energy Transfer Partners are operating under; and they are precisely what underlies the exploitation and degradation of the planet through the burning of fossil fuels. Cultural appropriation, is stealing, it is taking without permission or understanding. We were informed that this was a camp of giving and of self-sacrifice for the common good, for the rest of humanity and all the creatures we share the world with. Thus, many of our beliefs and practices that people came to camp with needed to be unlearned and ceased because they are components of the very things that brought us to Oceti Sakowin in the first place and what we are working to overcome and evolve beyond.

Oceti Sakowin Camp embodies the aspirational way of life many of us are striving towards. A world in which the first thought is how I can fulfill the needs of others around me, instead of being how I can take care of my own needs by extracting things from others.

Living among the people at Standing Rock I learned that I do not need everything I think I need in order to not only survive, but to thrive healthily and to be happy.

When everyone is giving, then there is no lack. There is no need to be fearful that the things we actually 'need' will be absent. This social organization is so completely contradictory to anything that most of us within the borders of Amerika are familiar with that it almost seems impossible because of how we have been indoctrinated to think and feel, but it works well. Not only is it liberating, but it is efficient and limits the amount of waste our society tends to produce and accumulate.

Many of our people suffer from forms of historical trauma, especially people of color. Some of us are also the beneficiaries of a long line of privileges gained from historical traumas, such as men and white folx, or both, and so the work to unpack, unlearn, and heal continues.

These are deep emotional and intellectual processes. As such, they are not easily overcome. In fact, we tend to bring these things with us even when we work to remedy human rights violations and to alter harmful practices.

Unfortunately, there were more than a handful of events and occurrences from which to draw examples from at Oceti Sakowin Camp. Notwithstanding that, and although it was problematic that a lot of misinformed, or uninformed, well-intentioned white folx poured into the camp during the week of Thanksgiving; it was nonetheless inspiring, to see so many people who are beginning to wake up and see our state of affairs for what it truly is.

That being said, there is no doubt that a lot of emotional labor was unduly placed upon our hosts and other people of color to inform, correct, and instruct a lot of the people who simply did not understand things like: it is not cool just to walk up and touch someone else's hair because you think it is fascinating. That is entitlement plain and simple, and it is an extension and an expression of colonization, one of the very things the people in the camp and elsewhere are working diligently to overcome.

Entering into another person's personal space, and especially touching their body without prior consent because of either an implicit or explicit belief that you are entitled to do so (and this includes rape and rape culture) is a colonial and patriarchal act. Consent is vitally important to healthy relationships. Firstly, consent signifies that there is respect between two parties and an acknowledgement of both their humanity and their agency.

*The Dakota Access Pipeline that Energy Transfer Partners is placing in the ground **without the consent** of Oceti Sakowin, is an act of colonization.*

They have come into Oceti Sakowin lands, desecrated their ancestral burial grounds, and threaten to poison both the land and the headwaters with faulty technology that in addition, will also promote the distribution of CO_2 from the burning of the oil, thus exacerbating the rate of climate change and the destruction of our environment. None of these outcomes are desirable to Oceti Sakowin, which is why they have gathered in opposition and put the call out for many forms of support. The Army Corps of Engineers, and Energy Transfer Partners have failed to respect the humanity and the agency of the peoples from Standing Rock, and by corollary, the rest of us. The reason that so many in our society, and even among those who journeyed to Standing Rock to stand and work in solidarity, embodied and acted through this colonial lens is because that is what we have been indoctrinated with.

Most do not understand that these everyday, seemingly minor expressions are what permit the larger, more broadly impacting expressions to exist and persist. Although, it is true that these things will not be overcome in a day, and that it should not be the responsibility of those who have already been harmed so much by this system and society of injustice to emotionally labor with those who still harbor, whether knowingly or not, colonial and patriarchal prejudices, ideologies, and beliefs, they must be continuously worked on; simultaneously within the system and within ourselves.

More than anything else, what I felt most while I was at Oceti Sakowin Camp, from the people at the camp, was love. Conversely, what I felt from the people in North Dakota who opposed the resistance to the Dakota Access Pipeline was sheer hatred and anathema. When I was abducted by the police in a most violent and unjust manner while the people were praying for protection of our water, the bystanders denied our humanity in a manner of which I have never felt in my life. I was accosted by a woman who stared directly into my eyes as I lay hog-tied on the ground in agonizing pain, when she proclaimed;

> *"Prison food is horrible. The way they treat you in prison is horrible. I hope you enjoy it there. You are getting everything you deserve."*

This was said moments before a chant for "blue lives matter," then a chant stating "oil is life" began. At this very moment, without restraint or regard for the welfare of people, the police were chasing unarmed, unthreatening, escaping, and innocent people—tackling them like linebackers from the San Francisco 49ers, slamming them into walls and doors indiscriminately; merely selecting people of color they thought might have been involved in the prayer.

In stark opposition, as was mentioned above, much of the spirit of the people in the camp was along the lines of seeking to establish and assert our own humanity. There was much forgiveness and grace, but more importantly, there was love. Criticism, when it is done constructively, and with the intention of improving the relations between relatives, is an act of kindness and love.

I suppose that is why when that woman looked at me with such disdain, and spoke to me as if I was not a human being, that I did not become angry at her or her actions, but instead, I felt pity and sadness, and began to pray for her. Ironically, and quite contradictory to my previous sentiment, I also prayed for the police officers as I prayed for our water, our people, and our collective future.

I am still not a fan of, and am starkly in opposition to, the police institution as it exists, the militarization of local law enforcement all over the country, the prison industrial complex, the school to prison pipeline, the counterinsurgency against social movements to achieve justice and equity, but something definitely shifted in me during my time at Standing Rock.

Although, most of us who made the journey did not do so to learn or take anything home with us, I do not think it is possible for a person whose heart is open to spend time at Oceti Sakowin Camp and not return home affected in some positive manner.

Many know that we need a new and redesigned legal and political system, which includes a new economic structure. However, more and more people are coming to believe that the actual shift must occur on a spiritual level and must spread naturally among us as if it were a scent on the breeze that we all become aware of. A spiritual transition is not something that can or will be motivated by force, it is more about attraction than promotion or proselytizing. It is slower, but much longer lasting.

When this manifests, then many of the officers, militias, and military personnel who, because of the authoritative structure and plausible deniability who feel secure in participating in human rights violations, may begin not to silence their consciences and moral aptitudes any longer, and may begin to question the unchallenged consent to execute unjust orders against innocent human beings. If it truly manifested, then those institutions would no longer be necessary.

The state will continue to issue orders, but the people will cease to follow them or step down all together. To be balanced, it has often been argued that the people in these positions lack consciences and that appealing to them is doomed to failure, disillusionment, and further repression. That has been the case more often than not, so this perspective is completely rational. I have stood with my people in front of a line of cops screaming until we had no voices left, dropping facts about the institution's dehumanizing and brutal actions, only to be beaten and unjustly arrested; and nothing seemed to change afterward.

So, I have seen it with my own eyes. Yet, there are cops leaving the force all over the country because the brutal suppression of innocent people is not what they signed up for, and police departments have made public statements in direct opposition to the Trump policy of racially profiling people to inspect their citizenship documentation.

Small steps to be certain, but it is evidence that a shift is also beginning to occur there as well. Like the Veterans who also journeyed to Standing Rock and participated in a major apology ceremony for their participation in the brutal suppression of Indigenous peoples, and made the declaration to oppose the practice. The indoctrination of lies and division that has sprung forth from Amerikan capitalism and imperialism is being torn apart and delegitimized.

Bernard LaFayette, the organizer from the Student Nonviolent Coordinating Committee, who went to Selma Alabama and began the voter registration campaign there, also believed in and practiced seeing the humanity of our oppressors. There is a certain healing power in it, and it is also pointing toward a future when we see and feel more points of unity than division and difference among us. It is my belief that this shift in cultural understanding is well under way and is spreading.

I felt more than the embers of this at Standing Rock, with people from all over the world, from many different backgrounds, with all kinds of stories all standing in unity under the leadership of the most impacted by this system, our Indigenous relatives. We all have much healing and growth ahead of us, and the state is ramping up its repressive regime, but it is inspiring to have witnessed and been party to the cultural shift of resistance that is underway, not only at Standing Rock, but all over the world.

#WaterIsLife

On Trolls and Safe Spaces

by Erica C. Barnett

"I am considered, today, so dangerous that today I'm the second most dangerous man in America—after, of course, Daddy."

"Daddy," of course, is Donald Trump, and the person speaking was Milo Yiannopoulos—the professional outrage purveyor best known for promoting Gamergate, getting kicked off Twitter for his racist rants against actor Leslie Jones, and signing, and then losing, a $250,000 book deal. Yiannopoulos spoke at the University of Washington, just hours after the inauguration of Trump, to a crowd of about 200—students and paying "VIPs" who made it inside Kane Hall before protesters outside blocked the entrance.

For those who made it inside the hall, Yiannopoulos' talk was a rare opportunity to enjoy jokes about "hairy dykes," "trannies," and "Sasquatch lesbians" while police in riot gear protected them from the diverse community outside.

It was, in other words, a safe space.

While Yiannapoulos cracked jokes about delicate liberal "snowflakes" who can't deal with the rough and tumble of the real world, protesters outside were getting pepper-sprayed, tear-gassed, and even shot. When word came down of the shooting, Yiannopoulos immediately pivoted to blame "the progressive left" for the violence, telling the crowd that it was under assault by "left-wing protesters with sharpened protest signs, with baseball bats, with flammable liquids, and, it sounds like, with firearms."

That wild speculation turned out not to be true; the man who was shot was a medic for the protesters, not a Milo supporter. The shooter, it would turn out, was a fan of Yiannopoulos. Meanwhile, Yiannopoulos continued with his talk—because, he said, "if we don't continue, they have won."

For someone whose "Daddy" has won the White House, Yiannapoulos certainly loves to play the victim. Like many on the far right, he claims to long for a halcyon past where men were men and women were "happier in the kitchen," neatly eliding the fact that men like him—pretty, vulgar, flamboyantly gay—were even more hated in that supposedly superior past than women who worked.

Yiannopoulos' own sense of put-upon entitlement and victimization plays well with fans who feel their right to dictate the terms of the world has been stolen from underneath them. He flirts with the deep-seated homophobia of the right by joking about volunteering for electro-shock conversion therapy now that Mike Pence is vice president, but he's a cartoon character, both fundamentally unthreatening and, in the actions he provokes with his hate speech online, deeply dangerous.

In person, he comes off as an insecure narcissist. Onstage, he's a kind of gay minstrel, applying lipstick and cracking jokes about sucking cock before crowds that would, likely as not, be more than happy to bash his head in if he wasn't mouthing the words they wanted to hear. His flippant misogyny and racism come across as opportunistic and insincere. His thirst for the spotlight is palpable, and he seems like he might blink out of existence if people stopped paying attention to him.

So should we? It's a classic question: Is it better to refuse to print noxious speech, on the grounds that reporting it only gives a platform to hate? Or better to expose it to sunlight, so that people outside the alt-right bubble can hear what its hero is saying and judge for themselves?

Well, I listened to the guy for an hour, and I think it's worth knowing what he said—if only so readers can get some sense of how the alt-right thinks. (Yiannopoulos denies that he's part of the alt-right, because, he says, he isn't a "white nationalist"—his mother is Jewish—but the former *Breitbart* editor exists firmly within the alt-right milieu, and he is closely associated with white nationalists and their fans even if, as he claims, he is not one himself.)

The crowd—overwhelmingly young, male, and white—laughed uproariously at jokes that would have been right at home in an Andrew Dice Clay set circa 1988. (Google it, kids.) A woman protesting Trump: "Sexually ambiguous super retard turbo lez." Rachel Maddow: "That nice young man." The fake roses on his podium: "Lena Dunham's seen more action. Well, actually, that's not fair, because she did rape her sister." Saturday's Women's March in DC: "Can you imagine 50,000 lesbians lost in Washington, D.C.? You'd be finding them in creases for weeks." The women attending the Seattle Womxn's March: "armpit-hair-braiding West Coast Femsquatches." On the spelling of "Womxn": "The 'X' is silent, just like their own ex-boyfriends are silent. Because they ate them."

You get the drift. Milo Yiannopoulos's juvenile act, conducted with a heavy assist from PowerPoint and a script on his iPad, consists almost entirely of tired, faux-"outrageous" jokes about women, particularly lesbians and "trannies," Muslims, and "cucks." For someone who's widely vilified as a white supremacist and neo-Nazi, Yiannopoulos has always targeted women with far more zest than racial or religious minorities.

Interspersed with the fat jokes, though, were a few genuinely frightening statements about specific women Yiannopoulos believe have wronged him, including Feminist Frequency's Anita Sarkeesian, one of the main targets of Gamergate. (Yiannopoulos relentlessly promoted Gamergate, the online and real-life harassment campaign aimed at silencing women who spoke out against sexism in games and gaming culture). Of Sarkeesian, Yiannopoulos said last night, "People don't hate you because you're a woman. They hate you because you're a cunt."

So what about Yiannopoulos's outrage performance art shtick appeals to the College Republicans who invited him to speak? It isn't funny, it isn't well-executed (a lot of the jokes failed to stick, in part, because Yiannopoulos drifted off on tangents, at one point literally getting distracted by a fly), and it isn't, strictly speaking, new. What it is, I think, is what has always passed for rebellion among young conformists—speaking "truth" to "P.C. culture," which is to say, parroting the racism and sexism of their fathers and grandfathers, even when they don't really mean it.

But there are real-world consequences to Yiannapoulos's seemingly harmless antics. He tells women to kill themselves, encourages his followers to harass women who cross him, and drives women off Twitter by inciting threats that make them fear for their lives. He loves to say that there is "no such thing as cyberbullying," but his online bullying has led to real-life threats against people—like game developer Brianna Wu, who had to leave her home after a Twitter user sent her "a string of threats including a pledge to choke her to death with her husband's penis," according to *Mother Jones*. (Wu, according to Yiannopoulos: "Another straight white male.")

The UW probably learned its lesson about interpreting "free speech" to mean "the right of anyone to use university facilities to say anything, at any time." (Then again, maybe not: A student told me UW President Ana Mari Cauce responded to her letter asking the school to cancel or move the event by saying that, hopefully, Yiannopoulos would decide to cancel himself.) But there's a lesson for progressives tempted to show up in numbers, too. Sometimes, even in the face of a loudmouth shouting insults, it's more effective to ignore the bully.

Pulling Together

by Minnie A. Collins

A twenty-seven-year-old waiter employed in a Yesler Street Hotel fell asleep in its lobby. Police came, accused him of loitering and beat him to death.

This was 1938. The man's name was Berry Lawson, a Black Seattle waiter. It was in line with the times, as back there were more than 2000 members of the Ku Klux Klan in Washington State.

They would meet on the 6th floor of the Securities Building on Third Avenue. KKK leadership condemned the *Seattle P-I* and *Time's* criticism of their actions and missions. Over at the University of Washington, the Canwell Committee held hearings accusing professors of "un-American activities". The hearings discredited and nullified identified professors' rights to freedom of expression upheld by the First Amendment of the Constitution. Some professors were required to take loyalty oaths.

Are not these past attitudes and actions as invasive as today's politicians' invisible health care, elections and tax proposals? Pitting people against each other? Keeping us distracted and acting out suppressed prejudices?

Time passes and lives change. Although Blacks have lived in Seattle's Central District for more than 130 years, demographics have changed. A population of two residents, Manuel Lopez in 1858 and William Gross in 1861, grew to 73 percent of the Central District in

1970. According to the Seattle Black population census, the total Black population for 2015-16 was 48,316 or 7 percent of Seattle's total population of 609,000. Why?

Seattle, especially the Central District (CD) is not a photographer's framed sepia print of Black contentment. Their assemblies of contentment were their churches, families, businesses, homes, and redlined neighborhoods. As long as Seattle's covenants redlined Blacks in and out, Blacks presented no economic threat to the status quo, caused no problems, and were small numbers, everything was in place.

As a 1956 resident of the CD says, "we had our own stores, bank, doctors, lawyers, homes and churches (*Seattle Times* FYI Guy). Black demographics posed no threat until the emergence of the railroad, Boeing's military industry, World War II, and shipyards. It was as though the industries became the stages for Blacks waiting in the wings for their cue and compensation in the labor market.

Up stage they were in the background. Down stage they demanded their civil rights. Demographic changes fertilized fears; economic fears caused riots; Affirmative Action fueled fears of Black privilege. Media, nevertheless, spread more fear as people tune in their ear to images and words that divide, destroy and demean Blacks in a city fearful of the "other".

Blacks continued to not only cope but also to coordinate alliances. They renewed and planed productive strategies among cross cultural and intergenerational assemblies for action. In the 1960s several assemblies, including the NAACP, the Congress of Racial Equality (CORE), the Central District Youth—which in 1963 staged a two hours sit-in inside the mayor's office, and Freedom School, organized and supported by churches, parents and businesses to protest the public school's curriculum: "business as usual in their children's education progress."

They assembled people power that provided sanctuaries and resources for families, friends and others moving to Seattle to earn better jobs, better education and degrees. Not unlike today for other migrants and immigrants seeking civil rights and economic empowerment and security for their families.

"Time and transition" photographer Inya Wokoma, says has created new alliances for decisive change in the Central District.

These new assemblies align across generations and cultures. Through local and global social media assemblies they are catalysts for revolutions. Their revolutions are positive because evolutions of attitude and actions occur; solutions can evolve in revolutions and revolutions cause change.

An example of cross-cultural communities and leaders who changed Seattle in the 60s and 70s are Bernie Whitebear, Bob Santos, Larry Gossett and Roberto Maesta. Their book *The Gang of Four* is an archive of revolutions in attitudes and actions for racial change, especially gaining civil rights for all.

W.E.B. Dubois, author of the classic *Souls of Black Folks,* states that the problem of the twentieth century is the problem of the color line. Yet, beliefs in a supposed post-racial society still exist to this very day, resisting the idea that racism is alive and well.

In his short story, "AD 2150", Dubois portrays a utopian society where a dead man, the main character, wakes up in 2150 and learns that human problems revolve only around the arts, nature, and human illness. The main character dies the same night! So too has post-racism died. In 2017, racism acts like a coiled viper, rising to strike out. Even ambushes its prey.

Today, much like in our recent past there are groups staking out alliances to combat this still existing racism, and doing it by wielding nothing more than the power of a device in their hand. Their smart phones give them "palm power" with which to meet, organize, and assembly briskly.

Among these current assemblies are leaders and organizations such as Rainier Beach's Northwest Tap Connection led by Melba Ayco teaches discipline, self-worth and family values. The Black Lives Matter movement rises to educate the world about a resurgence of mass killings of young Black men as well as the deconstruction of their families and communities.

And in this they have highlighted deep rooted needs of the black community: affordable/low income housing, gun control, rehab rather than prison sentences, education funding, job and voter registration training. Addressing some of these needs locally have been mayoral candidate Nikkita Oliver and the People's Party. Choosing not to accept corporate donations from lobbyists has helped her avoid payback for favors.

Her leadership has been joined by the likes of WyKing Garrett, of the Africa Town Community Land Trust, initiated assemblies of partners: Doris Koo, Yesler Community Collaborative; Forterra, land conservation group; and Lake Union Partners to own land at MidTown Center on 23rd and Union in Seattle.

Coalitions and partnership among Centerstone, Capital Hill Housing, Black Community Impact Alliance have led to the June 19 "Juneteenth" ground-breaking of the Liberty Bank Building apartments. On this site was Liberty Bank, (1968-88) the first Black owned bank in the Pacific Northwest cofounded by an assembly of multicultural leaders.

Because of redlining and housing covenants, Blacks could get loans only from Liberty Bank. Now on this site in 2018 will be 115 "affordable" homes and commercial spaces for local Pan-African businesses. All are partnerships for home ownership and economic renewal. Aligned with these assemblies is Black Dot Entrepreneur Epicenter which provides business workshops and co-working spaces for novices and start-up businesses.

Cross-cultural and intergenerational alliances and assemblies connected at the speed of light through their palm powers are focusing on economic sustainability, job training, and political participation in the Central District.

These partnerships provide employment for minority contractors, along with revitalization of black owned businesses, and provide home ownership for Blacks in the CD. Successful progress requires pursuing and participating in local and global assemblies of decision making tables and voting for candidates who represent community needs. "Harambee: All pull together."

The Crackdown on Immigrants and Refugees — What About the Children?

by Nakeesa Frazier-Jennings

Since writing an article about how Trump Administration's crackdown on immigrants and refugees is everyone's problem, I have continued to find ways to support my immigrant and refugees community members.

I've coordinated Know Your Rights Trainings, referred families to local agencies for assistance, attended trainings myself to become more versed in the many challenges that my immigrant and refugee committee members face and try to keep up with the ever-changing political climate. Now, I am beginning my journey to advocate for the children who are or will be left behind when their parents are detained or deported.

As a prospective adoptive parent, I have spent many years learning as much as I can about the adoption process. I've read countless articles, attended seminars and conferences, spoken to current and former foster and adoptive parents and more!

Recently, I read an article in the *South Seattle Emerald* that talked about a new outreach program that Seattle-based agency Amara was about to launch specifically for prospective African American foster parents. Due to my background in human services and preparing for my own adoption journey, I was already aware of the data that shows that foster and adoptive children who are placed in homes where there is a cultural match tend to have better outcomes than children who do not. Yet, just as in many systems, there is a shortage of African American families who are either licensed foster parents or have shown interest in adopting a child.

In a perfect world, there wouldn't be any differences between human beings based on their race, ethnicity, culture, etc. but unfortunately, at this time in our society, there is. That is a fact. So, recently, I've started working with Amara on their outreach advisory council to help create a robust program that will do all the things necessary to get African American children into homes with parents who look like them.

But what does that have to do with the immigrant and refugee community? Well, actually, quite a lot. There are many local families in the Greater Seattle/Western Washington area who are African immigrants and they are being targeted for detainment and deportation. Many of these families have minor children who are citizens and are left behind when their parents are detained.

I've previously spoken about how safety planning is important for our immigrant and refugee neighbors. Part of a thorough safety plan is to have people listed that a parent would want to care for their child or children in the event that they are detained (or deported). Since anyone can be detained indefinitely BEFORE even having a deportation hearing, it is critical that immigrant and refugees who are also parents have trustworthy friends, family or community members who can care for their children while they are away.

It is also critical for the children to be in safe, secure homes where they can receive the many types of support that they will need after losing their parents even if the loss ends up being temporary. A race, language, spiritual and culture match would be the most ideal in a less than ideal, and sometimes even tragic situation. So, I have asked Amara to incorporate not only American-born African American families into their outreach efforts but also African immigrant and refugee families.

My hope is that we will be able to help more immigrant and refugee families become licensed foster parents so that they can more seamlessly accept children from their community into their homes. We, as community, need to be proactive rather than reactive since we have no idea how long the focus on our immigrant and refugee neighbors will be.

Please remember, not only is the immigration and refugee issue in this country everyone's issue, we all need to remember the children of these community members who are innocent and are left without parents which is tragic and traumatizing. We must do what we can to try and lessen the trauma by supporting the foster and adoption system.

The Journaling of a Movement

by Donte Felder

October 12, 2016

Dear Journal,

I am shocked that the SEA (Seattle Education Association) Representative Assembly voted unanimously to endorse a collective statement that Black Lives Matter. I'm also cautiously optimistic that Seattle Public Schools (SPS) got on board and has also endorsed the day of "Solidarity" by proclaiming, "We stand united in eliminating the opportunity gap." I hope SPS' endorsement of the BLM is sincere and they are using the platform to create momentum in hiring more teachers of color, develop more relevant, culturally diverse curriculum, invest in the arts and more play time for students which promotes a growth mindset, 21st century skill sets, critical thinking and builds empathy for others, (Students of color are the ones mostly impacted by funding cuts to the arts and less recess to raise test scores) and shift your ethos from an outdated, industrial age, one-size-fits all approach, test-driven approach to an education model that teaches to human spirit and

Carpe diem!

Please don't go back to doing the same ol' thing SPS! This is the time to step up! Transform the negative image, mistrust, and adversarial relationship you have created with the African-American community. This is the time for a makeover—Get rid of the stigma that SPS can't teach black kids. Yes, you were called out by the *Seattle Times* when they said, "Seattle, among the 200 biggest school districts in the U.S., as having the fifth-biggest gap in achievement between black and white students." But if we do this right, we can become the model district instead of the "black" sheep of the education model.

October 13, 2016

I am having serious trouble sleeping tonight. . . . I'm thinking a lot about my complicated relationship with SPS.

I did hard time in the Seattle School Prisons aka Seattle School Systems for thirty-six years as a student and guard (Teacher). I was sentenced to the special education for five years during my elementary years and served my probation in the general education setting during my middle and high school years.

How the hell did I make it through as a black male with "special needs" in writing? The sad reality is only a third will ever exit the special education program and many will not attend college, so what inspired me to pursue a degree a MFA in writing.

I, like most of the brown folks in the SPS, particularly in special education, did not have teachers who looked like them or believed that they would amount to anything. The expectations for brown kids were low, many teachers were not equipped and did not have the tools or training to teach children of color. I also saw little to no representation in history books or great western literatures we were forced to read. The folks that looked like me often were marginalized and reduced to an inconsequential footnote about slavery or MLK. I never learned about the great inventions and contributions of my African-American ancestors. I was never exposed to the daring poets, authors, and playwrights that provided commentary on black life . . . I was made to believe that I was inferior, that I did not matter . . . that my people did not matter. I'm still struggling with PTSD . . . The culturally incompetent curriculum that SPS used back in the day caused trauma and self-esteem issues for thousands of students who looked like me.

But as hopeless and dysfunctional as SPS has been for decades, October 19 offers hope for a district that has and is failing its students.

I can do my part and hopefully and create a kick ass lesson that inspires the students in my class.

> "You build on failure. You use it as a stepping stone. Close the door on the past. You don't try to forget the mistakes, but you don't dwell on it. You don't let it have any of your energy, or any of your time, or any of your space." ~Johnny Cash

October 17, 2016

Dear Journal,

I am feeling good and sleeping much better now that I know SPS is for real! They are not preaching empty rhetoric but are truly committed to eliminating the opportunity gap. I was reminded what was written in the union contract referencing the opportunity gap, "There is not the luxury of time each day that passes without every effort being made to insure that all students can reach the standards set by the SPS for every student to be able to know and do upon graduation is a breach of our collective responsibility to provide a quality education."

Dr. Larry Nyland, Seattle Public School's Superintendent told the Black Christian News Network that, "eliminating the opportunity gaps really is the issue of our time." SPS also created the African-American Male Advisory Committee to address the needs of African-Americans males through systemic practice. The folks with the expensive suits are moving with urgency.

Black Lives Matter on the streets.

Black Lives Matter in the classroom.

And why am I getting writer's block now. I don't want to be the guy talking junk and can't deliver an Oscar winning lesson!

October 18, 2016

I have few ideas for my lesson tomorrow in my film and theater academy at Orca K-8 . . . What if I could help students understand that as writers, filmmakers, journalists, and storytellers they could have more influence on black lives than the activists in the BLM movement, teachers wearing a shirt, curriculum developers, or ineffective policy and decision makers . . . What if students understood the power of storytelling and developed the ability to write complex characters that reflect all cultures, races, and creeds?

How can I get them to understand that in our current political climate, art is just as important as activism? That these days the government is silencing journalists, and the police are shutting down protests, but they can still hide their defiance in their art. How can I get them to understand the power of cloaking meaning in metaphor? Should I teach students how conditional and implicit biases influence a frame of reference that criminalizes African-Americans? Should I narrow the lesson down and teach about micro-aggressions?

Maybe students should write a thesis paper about why there are so many police shootings of unarmed African-American men? I could spend a day or a week or a month or a year teaching them about systemic sexism and institutionalized racism and give them all the knowledge to teach them how the world is setup to keep them down. But sometimes, instead of teaching them how they're imprisoned, I think I'd rather teach them how to be free. Students have the power to flip the script. Stories will play a vital role in changing the negative perceptions and interactions with African-American men.

Historically, Hollywood has populated their films with stereotypes that indirectly influence our social interactions. It is imperative that more stories are developed that truly reflect the lives we lead, not the fantasies some desire. Imagine how much more powerful our movies, plays, and TV shows could be if only we put the authentic storytellers in place to tell the stories. Do my students know their own power? Have I done enough to make that clear?

October 20, 2016

Dear Journal:

It went down yesterday! Seattle teachers looked good rocking their BLM shirts! The support we received from the community was fire; tremendous, freaking brilliantly fantastic! Students walked in the schools with swag adorned in black, wide smiles and signs that exclaimed, "Black Lives Matter!" Hundreds of parents asked how they could support the cause, many organizations echoed the words, "In solidarity."

This day could be the day that shifts the narrative of African-Americans marching through the school-to-prison pipeline.

This current moment in Seattle history could be the catalyst for transformational changes to institutional policies, pedagogical practices, and myopic curriculum that has limited students' imagination and their historical knowledge of one-self and diluted their awareness and empathy for the experience of the other. This could be the day where institutions turn their empty rhetoric, broken promises, and foggy interpretation of equality into a city-wide action, a rallying cry for change.

I believe in you Seattle Public Schools!

We can do this together!

The Kids Are Alright, For Now

by Kris Kendall

At work on Wednesday, a palpable gloom thickened the air. I don't know the political leanings of all my coworkers, but it was easy to spot those disheartened or shocked by the outcome of the election. We shared stories of Election Day parties that went from cautious optimism to teary wake as the exit poll numbers showed what is now the stark reality: President Trump.

Being a Wednesday, I was due at the Lake Washington Apartments that evening to work for an hour with one of my students at the Youth Tutoring Program (YTP). Many of the kids enrolled at that location are from immigrant or refugee families. Many are of the ethnicities and faiths that Trump has disparaged, criticized or openly threatened with deportation—girls and boys who came here with their parents seeking safety and a future.

During the 2012 election, I volunteered for the YTP summer session and worked with three preteen boys: two from Somali Muslim families, the third with roots in Central America.

We were doing a project about the election and they asked who I was going to vote for. Curious as to what they would say, I asked: "Who do you think I would vote for?"

"Romney" they said in unison.

"What makes you think I'd vote for Romney?"

There were screwed-up smiles and nervousness as each of them tried to figure out how to answer.

"Because you're white," said one of the boys.

"You have the same hair!" Said another, laughing.

Okay, first that hair comment. Ouch. But I laughed along with them and we discussed the candidates, why skin color has no bearing on how you vote, and how I'm really going for more of a Jimmy Stewart thing, but whatever.

Back to Wednesday night, the day after the 2016 election. The student I work with on Wednesdays takes a specific joy in criticizing Donald Trump—especially his hair. And I fully anticipate he'll have something to say about the election results. But he doesn't bring it up. I don't hear any of the kids talking about it. From what I observed, the children treated it like any other night at the center.

So I ask as my student: "What do you think about the elect—"

"Don't even say his name," he says, cutting me off.

Our exchange barely goes beyond that before we're back to homework and fidgety asides about his sports heroes.

At the suggestion of our center supervisor, I'd read a *Huffington Post* piece with recommendations on how to talk to children who are anxious about the future now that Trump will be in the Oval Office. I haven't had a chance to try any of those ideas yet. Perhaps on Monday when I work with my other student, who, like many of the kids in the Lake Washington Apartments tutoring program, is a Somali Muslim. He too has a keen awareness of this election.

How will I answer him, or any of the other students there, if they ask how a man can rise to the nation's most powerful office with a campaign steeped in xenophobia, misogyny, and fear-mongering? I can't drag my feet and mope—there's plenty of that happening at my day job where the adults feel a sense of freedom to let the aftershock continue.

Eventually the topic will come up. Because these kids are curious, they're aware, and they know the tutoring center is a place where it's okay to ask big questions. This will shape their worldview. And I want that worldview to have more hope than fear, even if the newly-elected leader of our nation won that position by using a litany of talking points from the playbook of intolerance.

At work, the mood is still grim. I'm part of a team whose reputation and value hangs on creativity, but few are feeling inspired. Still, there are deadlines to meet and projects to complete. Yet at the tutoring center, just one day after we chose our new president, it was an oddly typical Wednesday. My student had a productive hour. I was happy for the distraction of algebra and Earth science.

The inauguration will happen soon after winter break. The other shoe will drop, and President Trump will be sworn into duty. I anticipate questions and comments from the kids at the Youth Tutoring Program. And I'll answer those as best I can, if I can. I don't know what I'll say.

What can any of us say?

With Automatic Voter Registration, I Can See Women Like Me in Politics

by Olivia Perez

Eleven days after my 18th birthday, I voted in my first election. That wasn't the only first: because my parents aren't U.S. citizens, I was one of the first people in my family to be eligible to vote in *any* U.S. election.

From a very young age I have wanted to run for office. I struggled to believe that running was a possibility for me because I never saw women who looked like me in positions of political power. I never saw Latinx representatives advocating for policies that would help my community or working to oppose policies that would hurt marginalized communities like mine—despite Latinx people making up the second largest ethnic group in Washington State.

As of the 2010 census, we accounted for nearly 12 percent of the population, and the numbers are set to grow. But in local and state government, we're barely represented.

As Washingtonians, we love to pride ourselves on our progressive ideas. Voting upholds all of them. It's the bedrock of our democracy, with the freedom to vote ensuring that every eligible person is able to participate in the political process, regardless of their identity.

But people of color don't receive that freedom equally, including the Latinx community. Many are migrant workers in rural areas. Many lead busy lives, juggling full-time, demanding jobs and family responsibilities. All of these factors contribute to low voter turnout and underrepresentation in government because of lack of structures that encourage participation.

Where our state should be leading, we're falling behind on a major voting rights policy: automatic voter registration (AVR). In the nine states with AVR, eligible people are automatically registered to vote when they interact with government agencies.

In states like Oregon, California, and even West Virginia, a simple trip to the DMV is enough to register a new voter with their consent. For people who move frequently, like migrant workers and young people, AVR is a simple, efficient solution for updating voter registrations.

AVR keeps voter rolls clean, accurate, and secure. Since the policy was implemented in Oregon, there's been an incredible increase in registration by millennials. I want to see that in Washington, not just for my peers, but for my neighbors and family, too. AVR is an essential tool to ensure that the freedom to vote is accessible to everyone—including Washington's Latinx communities.

Today, when I think about running for office, I think about women of color like Rebecca Saldaña and Pramila Jayapal who are currently serving. I think about the voters who elected them into office. Low voter turnout hurts our community: Latinx people account for 6.6 percent of all eligible voters in the state, but only 4.7 percent are registered, and we made up only 3.7 percent of all ballots cast in 2016's general election.

When registration isn't accessible, we're less likely to vote; when we don't vote, we don't elect Latinx representatives who know us and will be accountable to us. With a pathway to more accessible voter registration, my neighbors, my friends, and my family will have greater access to the ballot. Our constant struggle to be heard will not be as prevalent.

In order to elect people of color into office, there must first be an easier pathway to voter registration for voters from marginalized communities. There must also be an easier way to keep their registration information up-to-date.

Voting is the best way for my community to be involved in politics, but we are in a constant fight to be heard by our government. Washington must work to diminish voting registration barriers. This state has been a champion for progressive movements and by passing AVR, Washington can be the tenth state in the country to create a more accessible pathway for voter registration.

AVR can increase voter turnout for communities of color. We will be better equipped to vote for candidates who will advocate for our communities. We will be empowered to have a greater say in what goes on in our communities and in our government. And, hopefully, when Latinx kids look at their representatives, they will finally see faces that look like their own.

"If We Can Keep It"

Sermon delivered on December 17, 2016
Madrona Commons, Seattle

by Eric Liu

How many of you have ever been to a United States naturalization ceremony?

If you've never been, I urge you to find one in town and go. There are few experiences more moving, especially the "roll call of nations," in which the applicants, who've already taken and passed their citizenship exam, are asked to stand up as their native country is called. *Azerbaijan, China, France, Kenya, Mexico, New Zealand.* When the roll call is complete the immigrants are told, "The next time you sit down, you will be Americans." They then raise their right hands, swear an oath, and become United States citizens.

It gives me goosebumps just telling you about it.

A few years ago, after we'd been to a naturalization ceremony, my wife Jená had an idea. What if we created a ceremony like that—with ritual and emotion and an oath—not just for immigrants who were becoming citizens but for citizens of long standing as well? A ceremony where everyone, whether they were brand-new Americans or people who'd had the dumb luck to be born here, could renew their vows?

We were in a meeting and Jená got up to the whiteboard and sketched an image of a revival tent and described this not as a swearing-in but as a chance to be "sworn-again." And so was born a little project of Citizen University called "Sworn-Again America."

We created a simple template for a ceremony— readings, remarks, and an oath—then primed it with a few great partner organizations, and put it out into the world. There have been countless Sworn-Again America ceremonies ever since, at public libraries and college campuses and military bases. At the National Constitution Center and Monticello and the White House. At Starbucks headquarters here in Seattle and at house parties across the country. With a few people or a few thousand, all of them reflecting—some for the first time—on the content of their citizenship.

As folks create their own ceremonies, adapting them to local circumstances, the one constant is the "Sworn-Again" oath we created. Let me share it with you:

> *I pledge to be an active American.*
>
> *To show up for others,*
>
> *To govern myself,*
>
> *To help govern my community.*
>
> *I recommit myself to my country's creed:*
>
> *To cherish liberty as a responsibility.*
>
> *I pledge to serve and to push my country:*
>
> *When right, to be kept right; when wrong, to be set right.*
>
> *Wherever my ancestors and I were born,*
>
> *I claim America*
>
> *And I pledge to live like a citizen.*

You'll notice a few things about this oath. It's non-partisan, of course. But it is not morally neutral. It contains a judgment about what it is to be a useful contributor to the body. And it's written in a way that applies regardless of your documentation status: for there are plenty of people in this country who lack the papers but live like great citizens, and plenty of people who have the papers but don't.

Today I want to talk about three commitments from this Sworn-Again American oath. First: *To cherish liberty as a responsibility.* Second: *To govern myself.* And third: *To help govern my community.* In unpacking these three phrases, I am truly asking what civic responsibility really means when the body politic is as unhealthy and corrupted as it is today. Let's start with the first phrase:

LIBERTY AS A RESPONSIBILITY

This sounds nice. But I wonder how many people in this country truly practice it.

To many Americans, liberty means, roughly, *It's a free country, man. Don't tell me what to do*. Or, to use more historically resonant language: *Don't Tread On Me*. This notion of negative liberty is deep in our nation's DNA. And that makes sense, given that the big bang of our nation was founded to throw off monarchical tyranny. The idea that liberty is the removal of encumbrance has a long and distinguished history. Those of you, my fellow civic nerds, who celebrated Bill of Rights Day on Thursday can appreciate this.

But a funny thing happened on the way to Trump Tower. We Americans forgot that real liberty requires more than just the removal of encumbrance. We forgot that a society cannot stand on rights alone. We forgot that only toddlers and sociopaths believe in rights without responsibilities. And we forgot that the colonists in the 1770s who made flags that said "Don't Tread On Me" didn't need to make other flags that said liberty is a responsibility because it was profoundly obvious to them. It was second nature. It was the very definition of adulthood back then.

Rights don't just come with duties. Rights *are* duties. Freedoms *are* responsibilities. Liberties *are* obligations. You figure that out pretty quickly when you have to sustain your own little outpost in the woods with little outside help. Historians like Garry Wills and Bernard Bailyn have written about the deep culture of self-government that existed in the colonies before 1776 and that formed what Bailyn calls "the ideological origins of the American Revolution." Over a century and a half, subjects of the British Crown evolved gradually and subtly into citizens of a new nation. They made assemblies. They made town meetings. They made common law. They also made, thanks to people like Benjamin Franklin, fire departments and libraries and public health organizations. That evolution was a byproduct of the unforgiving environment: of having to figure out how not to die, and realizing that mutual aid and strong reciprocity and a code of responsibility are as necessary to liberty as oxygen is to flame.

It's the same lesson the Americans of 1787 had to re-learn when they faced the collapse of the Articles of Confederation and decided they had to ratify a Constitution to form a more perfect Union. Without that Constitution, each state was like a toddler, asserting rights and evading responsibilities and paying no heed to a continental tragedy of the commons. The states had to grow up if they wanted liberty to mean anything in the United States. The alternative, they knew from a decade of experience, was not utopia but bedlam.

The story goes that when Ben Franklin walked out of Independence Hall in Philadelphia after the Constitutional Convention was over, a woman passing on the street asked him what the convention had created. He replied: "A republic, if you can keep it." In other words: "We didn't create anything. It's on *you*."

And so here we are today. Hardly anyone talks like this now. The closest you get, in our militarized post-9/11 age, is the slogan "Freedom isn't free." I remember one recent summer during Seafair, when my family went down to Lake Washington to watch the Blue Angels —and I do appreciate the Blue Angels—and as those fearsome FA-18s buzzed past, a beer-drinking man with skulls and tanks on his T-shirt screamed out to no one in particular, "YEAH BABY!! FREEDOM AIN'T FREE!! WOO-HOOOO!"

But *this* articulation of the idea has more in common with the late Roman empire than it does with the early Roman republic—or the American republic that we were supposed to keep. *This* articulation of the idea is simply a reminder that our professional warriors—the 1 percent of our population to whom a morally avoidant nation has subcontracted a decade and a half of war, when we all should have been drafted and all should have served—that these warriors now have semi-sacred status as guardians of our liberties.

The natural conclusion of *this* articulation of the idea—freedom ain't free, so show respect to your military—is a presidential cabinet overstocked with generals.

No, I'm talking about the *Founders'* articulation of the idea. *Liberty as responsibility.* And I'm talking about their knowledge, as Bernard Bailyn wrote, that "free states are fragile and degenerate easily into tyrannies unless vigilantly protected by a free, knowledgeable, and uncorrupted electorate working through institutions that balance and distribute rather than concentrate power."

A free, knowledgeable, and uncorrupted electorate. Well, we have catastrophically failed in our responsibility to be *that*. The American electorate today is half-absent and the other half is half-ignorant.

Each passing day confirms that Donald Trump is a menace to our form of self-government. But in a sense, he is also a blessing. For in this odious, cynical, incurious, pathological person now *personifies* all the sicknesses in our political culture: rampant materialism and celebrity-worship, profound ignorance of history and the world, disregard for fact or fairness, addiction to instant gratification. He is not the cause of our democratic sickness. He is the result of it. (Although he may yet cause our collapse).

And what Donald Trump does for *all* of us is force us to ask whether we, too, are the personification of all the sicknesses in our political culture. How should we, civic physicians, heal *ourselves*? Which brings me to the second commitment of our oath:

TO GOVERN MYSELF

What does this mean?

Well, it means first, to remember that society becomes how *you* behave. Every social change, welcome or unwelcome, begins with the individual. Your choice to be compassionate or not, civil or not, courageous or not, becomes rapidly, immediately, imperceptibly contagious. To realize that society becomes how you behave is to leave behind the myth of what economists call "externalities"—the idea that you don't have to bear the costs of your bad or selfish behavior. But to realize that society becomes how you behave is also to leave behind the myth that you are just one in a billion, one helpless inconsequential individual. You are at *all* times a node of contagion.

That is especially true in *these* times—times when prosocial moral norms are teetering and when the people threatening those norms most vividly have titles like "president-elect" and "senior counselor to the president-elect." Those men have chosen to govern themselves a certain way, which is to indulge the darker demons of their nature, and they've given permission to many millions to act just as deplorably.

You—we—must generate the counter-contagion. We must create a countervailing kind of permission. Permission to speak truth to power. Permission to disrupt the disrupter-in-chief and to answer his cynicism and self-dealing with integrity and moral clarity. Permission to show some guts and to spend some capital and clout, if you have any, on behalf of those who have less.

For instance: How on earth did all those tech sector titans like Jeff Bezos and Sheryl Sandberg and Brad Smith go to the meeting that Trump called this week without one of them saying one word to decry the odious things Trump has said and done against women, immigrants, labor leaders, and everyday citizens? Those tech titans, each with their vast hoards of capital of every kind, were profiles in cowardice this week.

Imagine if all of them—if one of them—had held a press conference after that meeting and said, with all civility, that while their meeting was pleasant and interesting, they'd told the president-elect and they were telling the public now that they would never be party to the construction of an online registry to round up Muslim Americans and that the president-elect's rhetoric this fall against immigrants was especially harmful to a sector of American innovation that depends on making immigrants feel valued.

We should not wait on our leaders. We should lead them. We have to be the ones who signal that we will disable any such registry by flooding it with all our names. We have to be the ones who make that choice in our heart, and then vocalize it. To carry ourselves in a way that is conscious of the power of example and the example of power.

To govern oneself means figuring out exactly what you believe and why. Doing this is hard. It will illuminate how challenging it is to apply your beliefs evenhandedly. It'll also reveal what principles you won't ever sacrifice for personal gain.

Let me confess, on the point about applying beliefs even-handedly, that these last few years I was not that troubled by President Obama's use of executive orders and administrative rulemaking powers to bypass an obstructionist Congress and Article I of the Constitution. Why? Because his *ends* were appealing to me: ends like protecting our undocumented friends from deportation, like protecting the environment from coal-fired despoliation. But now that it's going to be President Trump using those same powers, I have a belated respect for checks and balances and for Article I and for the reasons why Congress and not the President was the focus of Article I.

If I'm to govern myself honestly, I must admit my hypocrisy about ends and means. And I've got to try to hold myself and my side to account with integrity. Because otherwise I remain too vulnerable to the temptation to sacrifice principle when the ends demand it.

I was reading recently about Elliott Richardson, an old upright Establishment figure who was United States Attorney General when Richard Nixon ordered him on Ocotber 20, 1973 to fire Archibald Cox, the special prosecutor investigating the Watergate scandal. In what became known as the "Saturday Night Massacre," Richardson refused the order and he resigned. His deputy, Seattle's own Bill Ruckelshaus, also refused and resigned. Finally, Solicitor General Robert Bork, third in command but least in command of himself morally, carried out the president's order and fired Cox. And Watergate approached its disgraceful endgame.

There are likely going to be moments like this in the coming Administration. But not just for Trump's equivalents of Richardson and Ruckelshaus and Bork. For you. And me. You want to be ready when that moment comes. It may not be in the White House and it may not be national news. It may be on your block, when someone emboldened by the times mistreats a neighbor. It might be at your kid's school. It might be at work, when good old boys feel like it's OK again to be politically incorrect and tell their female colleague how much they like the way she walks. To govern yourself is to know yourself morally. To know what will come out under the crucible of a crisis or in a random revealing moment. To know that you'll know right from wrong when the pressure's on.

To govern oneself also means regulating your behavior and your reactions to things. You can't control what Donald Trump does. But you can control how you react to what Donald Trump does. For starters, let's stop jumping at everything that little man tweets, or at everything that someone posts about what that little man tweets. In fact, let's take a social media Sabbath. Let's *decelerate*. Trump thrives on relentless acceleration, on creating a whirlwind of controversy that obliterates memory and disorients us from fact and truth and gets the body politic so stressed out and hopped-up that it's in a state of constant agitation that's like an autoimmune disorder. To govern oneself means saying no to all that. Taking control of your own metabolism and mind.

To govern oneself also means to experiment relentlessly in search of a better way to be of use to others. Mohandas Gandhi titled his autobiography *Experiments with Truth*. I love that title. I love the idea that to live like a citizen is to be running experiments all the time, personal experiments that may be invisible to all, in pursuit of a truer and better way to live out your ideals and to enact justice.

When Gandhi was a young lawyer still in his native South Africa, he wrote a letter to the great Russian novelist Leo Tolstoy seeking advice on how to liberate India. Tolstoy's answer cut right to the chase. Describing how the British East India Company had come to take over India, Tolstoy wrote: "A commercial company enslaved a nation comprising two hundred millions. Tell this to a man free from superstition and he will fail to grasp what these words mean. What does it mean that thirty thousand people, not athletes, but rather weak and ordinary people, have enslaved two hundred millions of vigorous, clever, capable, freedom-loving people? Do not the figures make it clear that ... the Indians have enslaved themselves?"

And after that wake-up call, Gandhi began tinkering with his own imagination, his own way of living, his own notions of convention and normality and what he would accept as conventional and normal. He began to see, as he later wrote, that "The moment the slave resolves that he will no longer be a slave, the fetters fall. He frees himself and he shows the way to others. Freedom and slavery are mental states." The rest, as we know, is history. But you don't go from zero to Gandhi after one sermon. (Even if it is crazy-inspiring to learn that Tolstoy lit the flame for Gandhi). And you don't leap from being a couch potato and Twitter addict to strong citizenship in one move.

So, finally, to govern oneself means to get in shape civically. That means setting goals and finding places to work out: *I will, in the next year, be able to give a five-minute extemporaneous speech on a civic topic.* Or: *I will organize (and meet) my neighbors to do something together for the good of the neighborhood.* Or: *I will, starting now, read national and local news every day, as well as trusted opinions from left and right.* Or: *I will, by midyear, learn what the core arguments are in American civic life.*

When you're civically fit, you can organize people through word and deed. You can recognize the patterns and the echoes from history when modern politicians argue, the way we now sense Hamilton and Jefferson reverberating in contemporary politics thanks to Lin-Manuel Miranda.

Of course, 'tis the season to be thinking about how out of shape we are physically and to make resolutions to remedy that. Well, it's the same civically. We commit. We pace ourselves. We make a routine. And the routine will go better and last longer if we show up with others and make progress together.

This gathering, at an hour when there is *so much else to do,* is proof of that. We are a community, and part of a larger one. So the final commitment we must make is this:

TO HELP GOVERN MY COMMUNITY

There's so much going around social media these days in the "What Should I Do?" category. The latest thing I saw is a document written by an anonymous group of congressional staffers—an insider's guide for everyday citizens about how to lobby and apply pressure on members of Congress to resist Trump's agenda.

I think this is exactly the right idea—and the exactly wrong arena. It's the right idea because every one of us now must become far more fluent in how power operates in civic life. Every one of us now must be able to understand in civic life who decides, who drives decision, and what gets left off the agenda for decision and why. Every one of us needs to learn how to read and rearrange the array of sources and conduits of power that comprise what we call the power structure.

To govern your community means to become literate in power—and to know how to read and write power. Too many of us know too little about how to make stuff happen.

But the congressional insiders' guide focuses on the wrong arena, I think, because the place for you, the citizen, to exercise your power and to achieve civic fitness most effectively today is *here*. Your community. That's partly because a gerrymandered and challenger-proof Congress is deaf to people outside each member's base electorate. But it's also because it is at the level of the city and the small town that we can learn anew how to run things like we are responsible for them.

Because we are.

Let me tell you, as someone who worked in the United States Senate and then the Clinton White House twice and who now serves on a federal board as an Obama appointee, that my true and best education in democratic self-government came during my ten years as a trustee of the Seattle Public Library, from 2002 to 2012.

In Washington the game was mainly talking points and positioning and the appearance of doing something. When you are one of five trustees overseeing an institution that's beloved by the city, there's no hiding behind talking points. You either build and program these neighborhood libraries in accordance with the hopes and dreams of the neighbors—or you fail to. You either learn who can make stuff happen in Lake City or Ballard or the International District—or you proceed at your own peril.

So take that insider's guide to Congress and apply it to City Hall or the School Board. Organize other people, your neighbors and friends and fellow Seattleites, for simple teach-ins about how those institutions work and how they could work better. And then, crowdsource a supplement to that insider's guide that's not about the formal institutions like City Council and the state legislature and people with public titles and salaries but is about the informal web of *who really runs this town.*

To govern your community is to know the answer to that question. Mayor Ed Murray is surely part of the answer. But so is Paul Allen, who holds no office but owns South Lake Union and the Seattle Seahawks and is defining the shape of this city's landscape and demographic profile. And so is Estela Ortega, who also holds no office but who runs El Centro de la Raza and is a power broker for immigrants and communities of color and the Beacon Hill neighborhood. And so on and so on. You can do a roll call of power brokers that is longer than the list of elected officials; it may leave many of them off.

To govern your community is not only to understand who *really* runs this town but then to insert yourself into the answer. To participate. To volunteer. To serve. To take leadership roles in established committees. Or to establish your own. The three greatest words in American civic life, words that Ben Franklin lived by, are *start a club.* On anything useful. To govern your community is to start a club or join one so that in the company of others you can practice power. And practice some more. And some more.

Now how, you might ask, will this stop Congress from repealing Obamacare or enacting Trump's tax cuts for the rich or doing worse? It may not, immediately. But starting and joining clubs, and signing up to make change happen where you live, rebuilds citizen muscle and it redistributes citizen power. Address homelessness. Fix mental health systems. Feed schoolchildren real food. Fund our schools right. And all that muscle and power can then be deployed in any arena, whether national or local. Sending emails to Senator X or Congressperson Y or sharing outraged posts on Facebook does not build power the same way or at the same rate.

It's not an either-or, of course, and many of us are simultaneously practicing power locally and applying what we have nationally too. As a people, we must all be in that spirit of tinkering and experimenting with truth and hammering out new practical ways to make change happen. Let an ecosystem flower from our diverse efforts. But wherever we choose to focus our energies, the thing to remember is what James Madison said in 1792. "In Europe," he observed, "charters of liberty have been granted by power. America has set the example . . . of charters of power granted by liberty."

If we in our liberty grant power to others to rule for a time, then we must also renew the covenant behind the grant—a covenant that says that they rule not *over* us but *with* us. *By* us. *For* us. The idea of a covenant has Puritan overtones, and covenant theology is what propelled the Pilgrims to Plymouth. But the American covenant belongs to us all. It's not just a Mayflower thing. And it is not a commitment to consensus; it is a promise to argue perpetually over the meaning of our creed. It is a hammering out of disputes and of often irreconcilable visions of the good life. It is a reckoning with dangers. It is a binding of fates that can be unpleasant and hard.

We agree to form and to reform this Union, to try to keep this republic, challenging and contradictory as it is, because we imagine that we are better off with it than without it.

A nation, Benedict Anderson wrote, is an "imagined community." That is particularly true of a nation like ours that has no mythic common bond of blood or soil. We are a nation bound together by the flimsiest thing in the world: a creed. But that creed, that cloud of intangible words like *liberty* and *equality* and *justice*, can also, when spoken together, bind our best selves together.

> I commit to using all my powers to resist authoritarianism in this country.
>
> I commit to teaching everything I know about civic power to as many people as I can.
>
> I commit to helping remedy economic and political inequality in Seattle.
>
> I commit to defending disfavored people whom Donald Trump tries to bully.
>
> I commit to building the kind of beloved community I want to be part of.

In a moment, I will invite you to reflect on what *you* are willing to commit to—and then to share those thoughts with each other over coffee and cookies. But I want to close this morning with the words I began with, the Sworn-Again American oath. These are words for friends. For neighbors. For citizens. I want to tell you during this holiday season, as we end a dark and challenging year, how grateful I am for the friends and neighbors and fellow citizens who give me and my family hope and strength. How grateful I am for *you*.

And so I ask you all to rise now, and join me in this covenant:

I pledge to be an active American.

To show up for others.

To govern myself, To help govern my community.

I recommit myself to my country's creed:

To cherish liberty as a responsibility.

I pledge to serve and to push my country:

When right, to be kept right; when wrong, to be set right.

Wherever my ancestors and I were born,

I claim America

And I pledge to live like a citizen.

Traveling Through Trump Country

by David Kroman

From Seattle, it's two hours until the trees disappear and about the same (earlier, maybe) for the voices on the radio to change as well. As fir and cedar give way to pine then wheat, local station hosts begin to warn of dangers apparently unknown west of the mountains. Israel, it seems, is in jeopardy, as is Christianity, as is your school and the place where you buy carrots or turnips.

I've made this drive growing up many times (hundreds, maybe). Once, because my dad enjoys the orchards as you descend on the other side. Another, to meet a dog I didn't take home. There was a move to Walla Walla and a drive across the country.

There was a baseball game. I've gone over the mountain pass so many times, I know, for example, that it's best to fill up on gas in North Bend, at the base of the Cascade Mountains, or it's a long climb watching the gauge all the way to Cle Elum.

I don't usually make the drive alone as I did last January. But I was on assignment. I'm a Seattle reporter and a Seattle native so, thought my editors, it would perhaps be a good thing to send me to find the Trump towns, the ones we heard so much about in the months after the election, wracked so badly with "economic angst" they'd apparently gnawed their fingernails down to the cuticle and found Donald Trump at the end.

My task was simple and one that hundreds of media outlets performed as well: We missed something when Donald Trump became president and it is maybe a good idea for us to find out what. Sending a Seattle boy would be anthropological, a sort of Dave Foster Wallace Goes on a Cruise Ship experiment, but with the weight of quiet panic inside my essentially non-Trumpian newsroom. The parents on staff especially wanted to know: Who put this man in the White House?

The character portrait of the mostly men, but also women, who put Donald Trump in power is the one of a white person who was once rich but is now poor. It's sheet metal, chain link fences, homemade brake drum forges, trucks with fumes leaking into the cabinet, grain silos, drawls outside of the south. It's painkillers and union halls with neon signs. It's styrofoam cupped coffee and Monster energy drinks.

And if I found those places and asked them about Donald Trump they would tell me, I believed, that for them the recession had not ended. And as I drank Budweiser I would listen as they explained how, for them, a table upside down was better than a table where they lacked a seat.

So I stopped in Ritzville.

Ritzville's economy is built on wheat and two highways that cross at its southeast end. It is not a rich place; Adams County, of which it is the seat, is one of the poorest in Washington.

There are two main roads running north to south, one on either side of a train track. The businesses smack of nostalgia: Memories diner, Pastime bar. A knick-knacks store that sells magnets shares a wall with a whisky distillery, done up to look like the old west.

Ritzville voted 75 percent for Donald Trump. Shouldn't a poor town that votes that way house the anxious voters we'd heard about second hand?

I started talking to people: the mayor, the city manager, a city councilman, a store clerk, my waitress, the owner of a coffee shop. And at first we would just talk, about nothing in particular. I learned that there is some tension between the downtown residents and the wheat farmers, who some claim live too well off federal crop insurance.

I learned that it takes decades to become a local in Ritzville, if you can get there at all. I learned the city was struggling to pay its bills thanks to statewide cap on property tax.

After some time, I began to ask about their votes; everyone I met had cast theirs for Donald Trump. It was here that I expected to hear about the anxiety of living poor.

But it didn't come, at least not quickly. The EPA ("a dirty word," according to one man) came up. The "swamp" and the people who run it came up. Agriculture came up.

And before economic anxiety, something else came up: Muslims.

The narrative about people who live in city bubbles, like myself, goes that we've missed something essential about life elsewhere, be it small town living or the impact of government regulation or the psychological trauma of being governed from afar.

Some of those are perhaps true, but it turned out the thing I missed most was how deeply suspicious some people were of Muslims, especially Muslim immigrants. Specifically, the small number promised entry from Syria by President Obama—10,000—dominated discussions and served as justification for electing him president. The words "Christian genocide" came up several times. One man suggested saving the Christians from Syria first.

It was only after Muslims that economic angst was raised as an issue.

Weeks later, back in Seattle, I would attend a meeting in the Central District's Seattle Vocational Institute. It was on police violence against African-Americans and was attended by a majority black audience.

While relationships with the police drove the discussion, it inevitably morphed into broader talk about how communities of color feel they no longer have a place in Seattle. The new jobs, new development, even new industry with legal marijuana seems to always leave them behind.

There are numbers to back up the sentiment. Median income for black people in Seattle is still lower than it was before the recession. Black home ownership is down. In fact, the entire black population is down. After eight years of a democratic president, African Americans in Seattle—no less a working class than the white people in the wheatlands of Ritzville—are worse off.

And yet they did not vote for Donald Trump.

There is cream on top of the jug of milk that is easily skimmed. The counties that voted once for Barack Obama and now for Donald Trump, whose factories have perhaps indeed shuttered: This is that cream.

But beneath that the well of people that elevate that final sliver on their shoulder, the people who are assumed to vote one way or the other and are therefore ignored in the analysis following a surprise election.

In Ritzville, there are people who simply vote Republican, be it Donald Trump or Mitt Romney: It doesn't matter. But my assumption that I'd find some economic anxiety there as a motivating factor shows how pervasive the narrative of a forgotten white working class has become, to the point that the storyline has co-opted opportunities for those who do not fit that specific demographic—like, for example, urban and black—to stand up and say, "But wait, I too struggle."

In my hotel at night, I could hear the train splitting Ritzville in two. The sunset on the edge of the long horizon cast long light on the loading docks and church steeples. And save for the oil cars and cargo trucks, it was quiet. And I could see myself there, buying land for cheap and watching swallows dart over sagebrush fields. I could eat at Memories diner or Pastime bar. The same people would pass me every day and every night and I would know who they were. Sitting outside my hotel door, I built a bubble for myself, one that, were it real, I may want preserved.

But when I woke the next day, I instead drove home.

Getting America's House In Order

by Lola E. Peters

Imagine that you're living in a very large house with ten other people who are not members of your family. Imagine that there are no agreements among the residents of the house. Everyone gets to do whatever they want, however they want, whenever they want. There are no agreements about the use or maintenance of common spaces: the living room, the kitchen, bathrooms, storage areas, parking spaces, or the garden. No agreements exist about when or how the rent or utilities are paid. Guests? There are no rules about them, either. Nothing dictates when residents can have guests, how long they can visit, or even if and when a guest is considered a resident.

If you've ever lived in those circumstances, and some of you have, you know how it plays out. It's not pretty. There are constant disputes over the use of space, cleanup, deadlines, and noise. Those who want no agreements often turn out to be either the least reliable and most disruptive or are the ones who are taken advantage of the most. Without accountability, there is chaos.

Whether you live in a household of two or twenty, the road to peaceful co-existence must go through creating mutual understanding. The first step in creating the agreements that bring order to a household is deciding on the principles that bind you, then defining a process that will be used to turn those into agreements.

Some residents may prefer majority rule while others want consensus. A few might even believe that those who contribute the most resources should have the most say in how the house rules are made. Deciding the core principles and process sets the parameters for everything that follows.

The more people involved, the more need to formalize those understandings, while simultaneously being open to new or adjusted agreements that fit the changes to residents' circumstances or needs of any new inhabitants. The formality ensures the process will be passed along to future occupants. For example, if someone moves out and the person who replaces them is allergic to certain cleaning products, a new agreement might be negotiated stating that all cleaning materials used throughout the house must be hypoallergenic. If a child is born into the household, new agreements might be needed around noise levels.

The flexibility of the process determines the survivability of the household. Imagine a household that came together in 1990 and adopted a rule that all telephone calls had to be made in the kitchen or that smoking was confined to the living room. How absurd would those rules be in 2017?

Once the agreements are decided, there must be a process of accountability. What happens when an agreement is violated? What's the structure? What are the parameters of potential actions taken against a violator? What are the parameters of benefits that accrue to those experiencing the violation? Who oversees the accountability of the violation and the process?

All households, regardless, have to face these issues so they the residents can navigate living in shared space. Imagine, then, a household of 325 million people, with no process, no agreements, and no structures for accountability.

Those who say they want small government are asking for fewer agreements (aka, laws or regulations) and fewer standards of accountability. They want no Environmental Protection Agency with regulations regarding how we share our water, air, and other natural resources. They want fewer laws about how we treat one another. They want fewer standards about how we share our physical space: where we build, the content or quality of construction, the way we behave in common spaces.

That housemate who wants to do "whatever I want in my own room" is letting everyone else in the house know that they believe they are completely autonomous. They are so self-focused that they don't see any impact that their private activity might have on the larger household. For example, smoking seems like a private act, but some of that smoke will seep out, either under a door or the moment the shared door is opened, eventually coating walls and furniture. Having a lover who stays over on occasion seems fine, but what happens if the relationship ends badly and the spurned lover decides to play a piano day and night in the park across the street until the couple reconciles.

I don't know most of the people I share Interstate-5 with, but we have some shared agreements about how we're supposed to behave while we're on the road. We agree to use turn signals to indicate a move to the left or right because we've learned that turn signals help us avoid accidents.

In the 1950s and 1960s enough people were killed by flying through windshields in car accidents that we agreed to use safety belts as restraints to keep that from happening. Each generation has created new agreements in hopes that more of us will be kept safe while we're hurtling down the road. This current generation, in the State of Washington, has added laws restricting use of cellphones while driving. As someone who has been rear-ended three times by drivers paying more attention to their phone than their driving, I'm grateful for that change, even though it's sometimes inconvenient.

Each household decides on its own process for making agreements. The selected process reflects the values of the people who are creating the household. If they believe that all members are created equal and should, therefore, have equal say in decision-making, they will create an egalitarian process. If, however, they believe that one gender is superior, then they might give the housemates of that gender more authority or more responsibility. If the core value of the household is adherence to a particular religious doctrine, the principles of that doctrine will dictate the process for making agreements. Whatever process is selected, it becomes the governing principle of the household, the core of its government.

Societies have presented many models for personal as well as social governance, ranging from theocracies, monarchies, and dictatorships to various models of democracy. The U.S. has adopted a modified egalitarian democracy, although there are segments of our society that still want households that are autocratic and who believe there should be one decision-maker in each household. There are even households who believe a particular religious doctrine should dictate the basis of our agreements. While this might work in a single household, the founders of the U.S. decided they valued a society of many religions and made that explicit in the language of the First Amendment to our Constitution expressly forbidding the use of any one religion as a decision-making process.

As a country, the United States of America made a decision that democracy would be our core process for decision-making, putting the responsibility on all of the people to decide the procedures and policies that would dictate how we share the land.

Generations subsequent to the initial writing of the Constitution and the accompanying Bill of Rights have reviewed and revised how we implement our democracy. Recognizing the exclusion of many groups, including women and then people of color, from participation in the democracy, amendments have been made to the Constitution to make it explicit that this democracy would meet its core principle: that everyone who shared this land would have a say in its governance.

Currently, we are engaged in an internal battle that exists on several levels. There are those who believe:

- they have the right to live autonomously without "interference" from the rest of us, despite the impact their actions have on others

- one religious set of principles should dictate the actions of everyone, and only those who adhere to that religious doctrine ought to have the power to make decisions

- that every person should have an equal, individual say in governance

- that some people are genetically incapable of contributing effectively to governance

- economic principles should dictate participation in decision-making because economic success is either (a) proof of a person's value to society, or (b) proof of special blessing by a deity

- the amendments made by prior generations should be rescinded

- whatever is best for the long-term health of the planet should be paramount in our decision-making

All of these disparate voices, and maybe more, are speaking at once, and it's damned hard to sort out the cacophony. If that tells us anything, it ought to be that now, more than ever, we need to be explicit about our agreements. In this era, we need clear agreements that are both enforceable and enforced. We need to be clear about our shared priorities, and about those things we leave to discretion.

The past 229 years have been about clarifying the agreements that were broadly stated in a constitution created to administer a population of fewer than 5-million people (including African slaves, indigenous peoples, and other non-citizens) who were spread over 13 states that all hugged the eastern shore of the continent.

As we've spread out across more land and the population has grown, so have the myriad needs of newly incorporated people and the changing needs of those already here. The core, driving principles by which decisions are made have been challenged and repeatedly revised to accommodate many changes. As our household had grown, so has the number and complexity of the agreements that we live by. How, then, do we continue to share this land?

It is inevitable that we have those among us who want fewer rules and regulations. I'm not among them. In my experience, the more open and honest people are about the parameters of how we live together, the better. In fact, it's the relationships with the fewest guidelines that have caused me the most pain and where I have caused the most pain. Guidelines provide clarity.

As with all things, there must be balance, and the way to achieve that balance is to begin with a deep assessment of the very process we use to make our agreements and ask if it meets its stated purpose. Does everyone's voice actually have equal weight? Is democracy the *outcome* of the process? Has it ever been? The answer is clearly, "No!"

We are in our current quandaries because there are people whose lived experience shows that their individual or collective voice carries no weight at all. How, then, do we rectify our mess? How do we get our house back in order?

The founders of the U.S. began with a set of shared principles. The process they chose and all the systems that grew from that process were all measured against those standards. The Preamble to the Constitution lays them out:

> *We the People of the United States, in Order to form a more perfect Union, establish Justice, insure domestic Tranquility, provide for the common defence [sic], promote the general Welfare, and secure the Blessings of Liberty to ourselves and our Posterity, do ordain and establish this Constitution for the United States of America.*

Are these still the ideals we aspire to fulfill? We know there are areas where these aspirations clash, there always have been. Do we have the moral courage to face those clashes respectfully and genially and work our way through them?

Our national behavior doesn't bode well.

We have become a winner-take-all society with no tolerance for nuance or complexity. We let the false narratives that came out of World War II convince us we were the world's best nation, and that we should always be seen as winners on the world stage. While even the most ignorant U.S. citizen will tell tales of "how we saved Europe, especially the French," few know that, at the same time, we intentionally sacrificed millions of Russians to Germany after promising we would stand on their behalf.

This adolescent need to be heroic has repeatedly played out in our insistence on defining other people's agreements and systems. Rather than allowing nations to work out their own way of government, we have repeatedly lied, cheated, killed, and destroyed their opportunities to do just that, while publicly saying that we're doing it for their own good. How would *you* feel about a neighbor who insisted you live by *their* household rules? Yet the U.S. public is repeatedly surprised when countries around the world oppose us.

So who are we really? Do we intend to adhere to the powerful words of the Preamble? Do our current agreements, the systems we have created to sustain and support them, and our accountability structures align with those principles? Are we ready to grow up and leave adolescence behind? Are we mature enough to admit our past and current mistakes and start on a path to bring our behaviors in line with our self-image? Are we ready to become a home, not just a household; a nation, not just a country?

The world is watching.

Afterword

What Now?

by Mark Baumgarten

My nerves are shot. It has been just short of 11 months since the election of Donald Trump and my brain aches with the fatigue of outrage. My heart weighs heavy. What another three years of bad behavior by our leader will do to my state of mind and body—or the world, for that matter—I can't say. We are in uncharted territory. I am certain, though, that my lifespan is being shortened one way or another.

So, yes, I share with all of the writers in this collection a sense of anger over the direction our country has taken since the new president's inauguration. But I am also different from most of the writers that precede me here in one essential way: I don't have to feel this way. It is, in a way, a choice on my part. Or, at least, it is not a state dictated by the circumstance of my birth.

I am, after all, a straight cisgender man with lineage that goes back to the fjords of Norway. And I grew up in a predominantly white community in rural Wisconsin, in a region that leaned heavily red in this last election. Under different circumstances—if I weren't raised in a family that encourages empathy and believes in the primacy of science, say—I may very well have celebrated the election of Donald Trump.

I think about this often. And then I think about how easy it would be for me, now, to just blend into the white patriarchy that has reasserted itself in these last few months, to become passive. I wonder if that fade has already begun. And I ask myself, *How can I guard against this?* The answer I have arrived at is a seeming contradiction and somewhat unsatisfying in what feels, more and more, like a moment of national emergency. It is not to stand out, but, rather, to stand back. And to listen.

So I am thankful that Marcus Harrison Green has collected these works by so many different people with such different experiences and different ideas about how to be vigilant in these times. Through these essays, I have come to better understand the emergency. I have been witness to the trauma that a campaign rife with bigotry inflicts on those in the bigot's crosshairs. I have explored the interior of the human psyche and the terrain of Trump supporters to better understand why that campaign succeeded. I have entertained reasoned solutions that aim to make sure that such a result doesn't happen again. I have read of rage and resilience.

Listening has provided me with a path forward. I have already used Lola E. Peter's metaphor of housemates when talking about what a functioning America might look like. Sharon Chang's intimate portrait of her family stands as Exhibit A for what is at stake in this fight for the future. And when I think of how we get to a better future, I now recall Eric Lui's words: "To govern your community is not only to understand who *really* runs this town but then to insert yourself into the answer."

But here is the thing with listening. At some point, it is not enough. The silence of the attentive, after all, sounds exactly the same as the silence of the complicit. Even the listener can be fooled into thinking they are doing something when they are just biding time, hoping it gets better before they are forced to step forward. The question, then, becomes when to act; at what point is it appropriate to stop listening and actually say something?

And let me be clear: We must speak up, especially people like me. We must stand against misogyny, against racism, against ableism, against xenophobia, against homophobia. We must volunteer to help the poor and the outcast and demand that the government do the same. We must engage in the conversations that acknowledge the sins that are at the center of our national identity and push forth a civic reconciliation that is far past due.

As an editor, I have operated for some time under the assumption that the solution to any problem is the right story. Recent history has not been kind to this notion. A substantial portion of our society appears intent on consuming lies while the rest of us are content to share a story and wait for change to come. Stories have seemingly lost their power. They have failed to set society on the right course. They have failed to keep government officials honest. This was evident during the campaign for the presidency. We knew who Donald Trump was. The journalists told us. And still, this happened.

I have not yet given up on stories, but I do not expect the right story alone to fix the problem. For a story to have any impact—for any one of these essays to bend the trajectory of our lives together—it needs a reader that sets the story down and stands up. Now is a good time to do just that.

~ *Mark Baumgarten, October 8, 2017*

About the Contributors

Rashad Barber

Rashad Barber is a community member and climate and racial justice organizer. He is a member of the Young Leaders steering committee at Got Green, and a member of the Seattle Black Book Club.

Erica C. Barnett

Erica C. Barnett is a longtime Seattle journalist who covers city politics and policy as a freelance journalist for various print and online publications and at her blog, *The C Is for Crank*. Previously, she was a cofounder of *PubliCola*, the local politics blog, a staff writer and news editor at the *Stranger*, a reporter for *Seattle Weekly*, and news editor at the *Austin Chronicle* in Austin, Texas.

Mark Baumgarten

Mark is the author of *Love Rock Revolution* and editor-in-chief for *Seattle Weekly*. In the last decade he has served as music editor of *Willamette Week* and executive editor of *City Arts, Sound, Twin Cities Metropolitan* and *Lost Cause* magazines. His words have also appeared in *Spin, The Village Voice, Seattle Weekly* and a few other now-deceased publications. Mark lives in Seattle.

Sharon H. Chang

Sharon H. Chang is an activist, photographer and award-winning writer. She is author of the acclaimed book *Raising Mixed Race* (2016) and is currently working on her second book looking at Asian American women and gendered racism.

Minnie A. Collins

Minnie A. Collins, author of *The Purple Wash* is published in *Raven Chronicles, Emerald Reflections, Threads, Crosscurrents* (WACC Humanities Association), *Quiet Shorts, Washington Center Newsletter, Washington English Journal,* and *Innovation Abstracts* at the University of Texas at Austin and *Blackpast.org*. Among her venues are Writers Read, a monthly program at Columbia Library, bookstores: Elliott Bay, Third Place Books-Seward Park, and Open Hand; the Hansberry Project, James and Janie Washington Foundation House, Northwest African American Museum, Columbia City Gallery, Onyx Fine Arts Collective exhibits, Seattle Public Libraries and Seattle Central College.

Irene DeMaris

Irene DeMaris is a public theologian, social justice advocate and agitator. She moved to D.C. before the election and is the Associate Director for the Center for Public Theology at Wesley Theological Seminary.

Donte Felder

Donte Felder has been a teacher in Seattle Public Schools for 18 years.

Nakeesa Frazier-Jennings

Nakeesa Frazier Jennings is a Self-Care advocate, race and social justice advocate, community driver, and artist representative.

Alex Gallo-Brown

Alex Gallo-Brown is a poet and prose writer living in south Seattle. His poems have appeared in publications that include *Tahoma Literary Review, Pacifica Literary Review, Seattle Review of Books,* and *City Arts* magazine. He is currently a writer-in-residence with Seattle Arts and Lectures' "Writers in the Schools."

Marcus Harrison Green

Marcus Harrison Green, is the editor-in-chief and co-founder of the *South Seattle Emerald*. He writes a regular column on South Seattle personalities, social movements, juvenile justice and American society. He is a former scholar-in-residence at Town Hall Seattle, a past Reporting Fellow with *YES! Magazine*, and a recipient of *Crosscut*'s Courage Award for Culture. He is the editor of *Emerald Reflections: A South Seattle Emerald Anthology*. He currently resides in Seattle's Rainier Beach neighborhood.

Mónica Guzmán

Mónica Guzmán is a 2016 Nieman Fellow and co-founder of *The Evergrey*. She is a former columnist for *The Seattle Times, GeekWire, The Daily Beast*, and the *Columbia Journalism Review*.

Renea Harris-Peterson

Renea Harris-Peterson is a Seattle-based student and social justice advocate.

Ben Hunter

Ben Hunter is a folk musician and community organizer who plays his stories through music, and talks about the communal role of folk music as a means to fight the growing trend of human disconnection. Benjamin graduated from Whitman College with a BA in music. With a passion for the folk culture, he has positioned his efforts around initiatives that drive that folk infrastructure.

Reagan Jackson

Reagan Jackson is a writer, artist, activist, international educator and award-winning journalist. She is also the Program Manager for Young Women Empowered. Her self-published works include two children's books (*Coco LaSwish: A Fish from a Different Rainbow* and *Coco LaSwish: When Rainbows Go Blue*) and three collections of poetry (*God, Hair, Love, and America, Love and Guatemala*, and *Summoning Unicorns*).

Marilee Jolin

Marilee Jolin is the Executive Director of the *South Seattle Emerald* and a former Junior Miss. She is an active member of the Hillman City Collaboratory, European Dissent and is the proud parent to two Seattle Public Schools elementary students (Beacon Hill International School).

Kris Kendell

Kris Kendell is a former journalist, and current Rainier Beach resident.

David Kroman

David Kroman is the city reporter for *Crosscut*. He grew up on Bainbridge Island and likes to canoe.

Kristin Leong

Kristin Leong, M.Ed. is a speaker, writer, and Humanities teacher. She once delivered a five minute performance at Town Hall Seattle entitled "Nightclub Bartending & Middle School Teaching: A Venn Diagram." Kristin is also an advocate for critical thinking across grade levels and student-led classrooms.

Eric Liu

Eric Liu is the founder and CEO of Citizen University and executive director of the Aspen Institute Citizenship and American Identity Program. Eric served as a White House speechwriter and policy adviser for President Bill Clinton. He is a regular columnist for *CNN.com* and a correspondent for *TheAtlantic.com*.

Hanna Brooks Olsen

Hanna Brooks Olsen is a co-founding editor of *Seattlish* and has written for the *Atlantic*, *CityLab*, and *Seattle Met*. When not stringing together words or making sounds she enjoys music on vinyl, bourbon, college football, making impulse purchases at second-hand stores, ballet, and sitting in dark bars with friends. She also sings a mean rendition of *Walking in Memphis*.

Olivia Perez

Olivia Perez is a University of Washington student and the first in her family to attend university. She is studying political science and labor studies.

Lola E. Peters

Lola E. Peters is Editor-at-Large for the *South Seattle Emerald*. She is an essayist and poet who writes about politics, religion, justice, art, and other forbidden topics. She has published two books of poetry (*Taboos*, and *The Book of David*) and a book of essays (*The Truth About White People*).

emily warren

emily warren is a Seattle-based educator serving students for more than twenty years.

Dustin Washington

Dustin Washington is a Core Trainer with the People's institute for Survival and Beyond and Clinical Faculty at the School of Public Health at the University of Washington. Dustin's work centers around developing humanistic, anti-racist leadership across the nation and beyond through the #NewWoke movement. He is the winner of numerous awards: Faith Action Network Social Justice Award, Fellowships of Reconciliation Martin Luther King Jr. Award and Seattle Human Services Coalition's Ron Chisolm Anti-racist Leader Award.